Ideas in Drama

Michael Theodorou

STANLEY THORNES
(PUBLISHERS) LTD

First published in 1989 by:
Stanley Thornes (Publishers) Ltd
Ellenborough House
Wellington Street
CHELTENHAM GL50 1YW
England

97 98 99 00 / 10 9 8 7 6 5 4 3

British Library Cataloguing in Publication Data
Theodorou, Michael
    Ideas that work in drama
    1. Great Britain. Secondary schools. Curriculum subjects.
    Drama
    I. Title
    792'.07'1241
    ISBN 0-7487-0225-3

Typeset by 🅰 Tek Art Ltd, Croydon, Surrey
Printed in Great Britain by Redwood Books, Trowbridge, Wiltshire

Contents

SECTION FOUR: VISUAL STIMULI

Introduction

This is a stimulus book. It does not purport to lay down rules about lesson structure or the theory of drama teaching. It is essentially a practical book based on personal experience and aimed principally at the hard-pressed drama teacher in a secondary school who is constantly having to think up ideas to stimulate his or her pupils.

The whole range of human experience is available to the drama teacher. That's the problem. 'What do I choose? How shall I select?' The answer is to choose stimulating ideas from the world around us that are suitable for our particular pupils. One idea might work in one school but not in another. Why? Because the right idea has not been chosen. But which idea? And how to make the connection? The answer is to know your pupils, to choose instinctively the right idea for the right age group.

If the drama teacher has no feeling or enthusiasm for the idea, it is difficult to elicit a creative response from the pupil. Yet we all know that, even for teachers, regularity can breed monotony, routine can give birth to apathy and enthusiasm can soon be doused by the hosepipe of daily, pedestrian problems. The drama teacher has no props on which he or she can lean like most other teachers. You can't say 'Turn to page 25 and do exercise 6.' It takes emotional energy to teach drama successfully, and batteries soon run down in such a highly charged atmosphere. The drama teacher's fuel is therefore – ideas.

Ideas in this book are presented with a particular age group in mind – though quite often an idea can be adapted to suit pupils of all ages. The tone of the book is that of a drama teacher taking an actual lesson. Each of the ideas contained in Sections 1 and 2 includes a suggested introductory speech with which the drama teacher can address the class. This can be tailored to individual needs and situations. Teacher's notes are also included; these are intended to be adapted for your particular pupils. Development sections follow; these can be used if thought appropriate to your needs. The best way to use this book is to select ideas that you think may be of interest to and may stretch your particular pupils.

This is the kind of book I wanted to read some years ago when I first started drama teaching. There seemed to be lots of books about 'why' and 'how' to teach drama but not very many about 'what' to teach. The book is also aimed at the needs of student teachers who are either studying drama as a specialist subject or as a subsidiary, especially when they are doing their teaching practice. Youth club leaders and teachers of pupils with special needs may also find the ideas in this book useful, as might even the experienced drama specialist who is faced with GCSE drama examinations. The text stimuli section is specifically for students at key stage 4, and the visual stimuli section will serve both the advanced student and pupils lower down in the school.

The National Curriculum ('Cox') report, *English for ages 5–16*, stresses the value of drama in the English curriculum, as a learning medium for the Speaking and Listening profile component. The activities in this book are designed to develop and broaden pupils' communication skills, and will be a valuable resource for teachers of English.

Finally, if I have a philosophy of drama, it concerns the development of personality. Young people should acquire social and life skills through drama. We endeavour to bring out positive aspects of personality: self-confidence, a tendency to listen actively, a sense of humour, the ability to relate more easily to others – possibly because one is more at ease with oneself. Drama is about instilling the desire to communicate. It is about losing inhibitions. It is about feeling the confidence to express your own point of view. In skilled hands it can be used as a positive and illuminating method of creating a more conscious and tolerant group of human beings.

This view is endorsed by *English for ages 5–16*: '[Drama] helps pupils express emotions and explore personal feelings; it encourages them to make sense of different situations and different points of view, to practise negotiating successfully with others and to cope with – and resolve – new situations.' Drama gives the opportunity of creating a more balanced personality in pupils at a crucial stage in their development. It is vital to the good health of both schools and society at large, which is why I earnestly hope that it will continue to be a force of importance in the curriculum. 'No man (or woman) is an island.' At least, not in the drama class.

Michael Theodorou

Working in large groups

1 Imaginary bomb :
• Age range: 11–12
• Key words: alertness, concentration

Get into a large circle. Make sure you can see everybody. Check that you know everyone's name. If you don't, ask them. This game depends upon you knowing other people's names.

I shall join you in the circle. I am holding an imaginary bomb. Here it is. I am going to throw the bomb to somebody in the circle and at the same time say their name.

If the bomb is thrown to you, you must immediately throw it to somebody else and say that person's name. If you hesitate, the bomb explodes and you are out of the circle.

If you say the wrong name, you are out. If you get tongue-tied you are out. If you say 'er' you are out. All you are required to do is throw the bomb straight away to another person, look towards them and say their name.

First of all, we can say first names and then we can change it to second names.

The bomb must travel very quickly because you obviously don't want to be blown up, so get rid of it, but do say the other person's name clearly, otherwise I shall have to eliminate you.

The last two people left are the winners.

(Later on I'm going to add another rule to make it more complicated: 'You can't throw the bomb back to the person who threw it to you'. But for the time being you can throw it to anybody.)

TEACHER'S NOTES

1. Have a few rehearsals before you start for real.

2. Insist on speed and be firm about asking people to step out of the circle if they are 'out'.

3. As soon as you find two people throwing the bomb back and forth to

each other, introduce a rule about not throwing the bomb back to the person who threw it to you.

4. This exercise is great fun for older as well as younger pupils and is a good way of starting a lesson, especially for those who need to be 'brought out of themselves'. It can also help you to get to know the pupils' names. Stand outside or inside the circle as you wish.

5. You can use the word 'game' to the pupils if you like, but really it's an exercise.

6. I sometimes say, 'Now I'm going to light the bomb, it's one of those old-fashioned round black things with a fuse at the top. Do you know the one I mean, like in the comics?' At other times I say, 'I've just discovered this unexploded bomb. It might go off any second'. Do a mime. Make them 'see' the bomb and insist on their catching it according to its weight and shape.

2 Bing bong

● Age range: 11–12
● Key words: listening, concentration

Get into a circle . . . no, that's more of a square. A circle please, a smooth circle. To get a perfect circle touch elbow to elbow with your neighbour.

Now I'm going to stand in the middle of the circle and point at someone. Or I might just call out someone's name.

If it's you, you have to say 'Bing'; the person on your right then says 'Bong'; the next person then says their own name, quite simply. The next person says 'Bing'; the next person 'Bong'; the next person their own name, etc.

We carry on until someone makes a mistake, then that person has to step outside the circle and wait till the next round.

I might change it to 'Bing bong bing name', so listen carefully to my instructions and also to your immediate neighbour's. You'll be surprised how many people think their own name is 'Bing' or 'Bong'.

Ready? The last person left is the winner.

TEACHER'S NOTES

1. As soon as you find that a pattern has been established, change to either 'Bing bong name' or 'Bing bong bing name'. Even numbers in the circle mean you should use 'Bing bong'. Odd numbers mean you should use 'Bing bong bing'. Of course you can add as many 'Bing bongs' as necessary in order to make it more complicated.

2. 'Bing bong' could be a bell sound or a clock sound, so suggest it to the pupils and ask them to 'sound' like a clock or like a bell when they are saying 'Bing' or 'Bong'. The name however must be 'straight'.

3. This exercise must proceed with speed and people must be eliminated as soon as they've made a mistake.

4. As a variant on 'Bing bong' I've found the following work quite well:

   Hee haw (ass or mule);
   Drip drop (water);

Plink plonk (piano);
Clink clank (chains);
Clip clop (horse);
Flip flop (shoes);
Ping pong (bell);
King kong (a big ape!).

5. Further complications can be added by telling the class that they must not say their own name but the name of the person standing on their left or right. This is an excellent game for breaking the ice with a rather reserved class and a fun way of ending a serious lesson with an exuberant class.

3 Jaws

• Age range: 11–13
• Key words: observation, concentration

Imagine that the whole of the hall/studio is an area of sea or ocean. You are all small fish swimming in the water.

One of you is to be 'Jaws' and must go outside. When Jaws is out of the room, we elect someone to be a human being who has fallen into the ocean.

When Jaws comes in, you will all be swimming but Jaws will not know who the human being is.

Jaws must watch very carefully for any sign or clue as to who the human being might be. There will be nothing to indicate the human being, therefore Jaws must 'feel' who it might be and go for them – 'jaws gnashing' as soon as he or she smells blood.

If a fish is caught, the fish makes no sound. Only the human being can make a horrifying scream when caught. The winning Jaws is obviously the one who captures the human being as early as possible.

TEACHER'S NOTES

1. You can use the 'Jaws' theme music for this 'game'.

2. If the pupils are finding it really difficult to identify the human being through the power of observation and 'feeling', then, as a clue, the teacher can turn up the music a little when Jaws swims near. The 'Jaws' theme can be tapped out on a piano if necessary, or on a drum or even a chair.

3. The teacher can also turn off the music or stop playing the piano. Then Jaws has to freeze but the rest of the class continue swimming. This will allow the human being to live a little longer. Music starts up again and Jaws can move.

4. There is no reason why a pupil cannot handle the music.

5. Absolutely no talking allowed.

6. A variant is to have the whole class as human beings, with one Jaws swimming among them and killing them by opening his or her mouth. The rest of the class keep their mouths firmly shut.

   A pupil is chosen to be shark hunter and goes outside the room. When the shark hunter is outside, a Jaws is selected and then the shark hunter re-enters and has to guess the identity of Jaws by observing who is doing the killing.

   Human beings must fall dead as soon as Jaws opens his or her mouth at them. Jaws, of course, must be subtle enough to open his or her mouth without the shark hunter seeing him or her.

4 Robots

- Age range: 11–12
- Key words: communication, listening, trust

Find a partner. One of you is Master, the other is Robot. The robot cannot see; it is blind and must be guided by the master. Instructions such as 'forward', 'left', 'stop' are to be used.

All masters must stand with their backs to the wall and must not follow the robot around. Instructions must only be taken by a robot from the right master.

The purpose of the exercise is to guide your robot through a narrow gap at the other end of the room.

If robots collide, they explode and are out of the game. So give very definite orders and, robots, listen very carefully to your master's voice – and trust!

TEACHER'S NOTES

1. Ask the pupils to arrange chairs with a narrow gap and practise their master/robot parts for a few minutes. Blindfolds can be given out if necessary.

2. Depending on the size of the class, you can have a knockout competition between three pairs with the winner going forward to the next round, etc. If you decide on this method, it is useful to have 'twisters' to turn the robots round in order to disorientate them before the competition starts.

3. If you want a competition, you can vary the rules by saying, 'The first robot through the gap and back to the master is the winner'.

4. When the game has developed a little, the masters are not allowed to use words but only 'sounds' to direct their robots. The pairs need to discuss and practise their sound or sound code before starting.

5. You can have as many pairs of masters/robots as space will allow. A suitable piece of electronic music can be used to add atmosphere: *Doctor Who* music or Stockhausen; anything weird and mechanical-sounding.

5 Dracula

● Age range: 11–13
● Key words: observation, group awareness

You probably all know the story of Dracula, the vampire, and his arch enemy Professor Van Helsing, the vampire catcher.

One of you has to be Van Helsing and go out of the room. Once Van Helsing is outside we decide on who is to be Dracula.

Dracula kills people by baring his or her teeth at them. If Dracula does this to you, clutch your neck and die with a blood-curdling scream.

Van Helsing will be called back in as soon as we have chosen a Dracula. It is then Van Helsing's job to guess the identity of Dracula.

Obviously Dracula has to be as cunning as possible, baring his or her teeth when Van Helsing is not looking. Everybody else in the class has to have their mouths firmly shut. Anyone else who bares their teeth is out of the game.

Dracula's aim is to kill as many people as possible before being unmasked.

Van Helsing's aim is to kill Dracula before Dracula kills everybody. Van Helsing can either plunge an imaginary stake through Dracula's heart or hold a crucifix up at him.

If Van Helsing tries to kill the wrong person, that person just keeps moving.

TEACHER'S NOTES

1. All the participants roam round the hall/studio, keeping their mouths firmly shut. They must not go out of their way deliberately to confuse Van Helsing.

2. You can tell the pupils exactly how they should walk, for example, in a trance, like zombies. Tell them to be aware of other people, watching everyone very carefully, being alert to what is happening, but having the self-discipline to keep their mouths shut and restrict their movements.

3. Another method of playing this game is for the teacher to select one

person to be Dracula without the rest of them knowing who it is. Either give out blank cards with one Dracula card amongst them or ask the whole class to stand in a circle with their eyes closed whilst you tap Dracula.

Anyone in the class can accuse someone of being Dracula at any time, but a wrong guess means instant death and being out of the game. The person who guesses correctly is the next Dracula.

4. I've found that this exercise in observation gains considerably in atmosphere by the use of music. Bartok's *Miraculous Mandarin Suite* is particularly apt. A lowering of the lights can also be appropriate.

Further development

1. Below is a suggested scenario for continuing with the theme of Dracula and the mood of eerie menace which children of this age generally love.

   Get them into groups of six.

   The title is 'Breakdown in the middle of nowhere'. The characters are mother, father, two children, zombie servant and Dracula.

   The car bearing four people breaks down in the middle of the countryside at night. (Where were they going or returning from?) The people see a distant light across the fields.

   They try to peep in the windows of a big mansion but all of them have shutters, except one room at the top which is where the light is coming from. They knock at the door (cavernous effect). Footsteps are heard descending a staircase (sound effects). The door creaks open and a weird head appears. It's the 'Igor' servant-zombie character. They explain what has happened and are invited inside.

   The servant leads them into the great hall. The master/mistress of the house enters and welcomes them, ordering the servant to bring food and drink. The drink is drugged and soon all the family fall asleep.

   Open ending. Ask the pupils to finish by themselves in not more than two scenes.

2. Instead of a car, suggest that they might use a carriage and horses (they can make their own sound effects again here) and make it into a 19th century Victorian-style play nearer to the original.

3. Another way of working with pupils' creative imagination is to ask them to 'mime' the whole scenario. No words at all. Just sound effects. Possibly in the style of a silent movie (with cards to indicate change of location and characters' feelings), but don't do this until they've had a thorough verbal run-through and have created the flow of the story.

6 Physical work— starting from a simple gesture

• Age range: 14–15 • Keywords: physical expressiveness, concentration

> I want you to imagine a camera is filming your hands in close-up.
>
> First of all, I want you all to rub your hands together as if you were very cold. The camera is slowly going to pull away to reveal your whole body and face.
>
> As you rub your hands together you are going to become a definite character in a definite setting. For example, you could be a tramp down by the docks around a rubbish fire, or a person locked out of their house in the cold, or an escaped convict on the moors.
>
> Ready? . . . and rubbing hands together . . . Go! . . . camera in close up . . . camera pulling away to reveal all of you.

TEACHER'S NOTES

1. See how pupils cope with inventing their own characters. They can all work at the same time, either individually or in pairs. Watch for physical expressiveness and encourage good efforts.

2. Now call out stimuli for hand gestures: 'tramp' . . . 'convict' . . . 'detective'. The gesture of rubbing hands also works well: (a) over money (Scrooge, Harpagon); (b) having done a wicked deed (witch); (c) looking forward to a meal, a journey, a good film, meeting your boyfriend/girlfriend; (d) washing blood off your hands (Lady Macbeth).

3. Suggest to the class the action of twiddling thumbs or tapping hands while someone is: (a) about to make a confession to their mother, a priest, a policeman; (b) thinking hard, about to make a decision; (c) daydreaming; (d) waiting impatiently for a train, the dentist, their son/daughter who is late, a boyfriend or girlfriend.

4. Suggest to the class the gesture of pointing with the index finger or wagging a finger: (a) accusingly at a murderer; (b) at a pupil chewing gum

in class; (c) recognising someone who stole from them; (d) telling off a child, a friend, an employee; (e) pointing the way along a road, up a hill, round the corner, to heaven, to hell.

5. Now move on to the action of raising hand(s): (a) to answer a question in class; (b) to volunteer for a duty eagerly; (c) to volunteer reluctantly; (d) to indicate how tall somebody is; (e) to touch the ceiling; (f) to lift a weight; (g) to hold up the ceiling; (h) on being held up in a bank; (i) to reveal one's presence to a helicopter, a distant ship, a friend across a hill; (j) to wave goodbye to a person one is glad to see the back of; (k) to wave goodbye sadly.

6. The idea is to develop physical expressiveness, to make the pupil aware that gesture is an outward manifestation of thought. Focusing on a gesture with an imaginary film camera concentrates the attention on a specific area before pulling back and seeing the whole character, i.e. the whole thought.

For many of the above gestures, the instruction 'freeze' could be used at some point. It is important for pupils to be made aware that body movement, however small, is linked to the whole person. People in many countries accompany their speech with a continuous movement of the hands, expressing thought. Deaf people communicate in sign language. Stress that words are not always necessary for communication.

Further development

1. Ask the class to get into pairs or threes and tell them to express to each other the following thoughts in gesture:

I'd like you to go away please.
Stop, you're going to crash your car into my hedge.
You told me to wait here until the head arrived.
I can't see the person you love, only the person you hate.
Can't you hear my mother coming down the stairs?
I can smell gas escaping. It might kill us.
The meal I had in that smart restaurant yesterday was awful.
You never do your homework, look at this report.
I'm really mean with money. I love to save and not spend any at all.
I'm begging you to believe that I did not commit the murder.
Yes, I'm ready to go on safari and then climb to the top of the highest mountain in the world.

Any temptation to speak must be firmly discouraged.

2. Ask the class to get into groups of four and devise a short improvisation which starts with a definite gesture (accept rude ones). The gesture has to be highlighted at the beginning 'in close up' before the dialogue even starts. The best method is to begin with a freeze frame and for someone in the group to call 'action' as the cue for starting the movement and speech. If they're stuck, suggest some of the following:

(a) palm of the hand raised in a gesture of peace;
(b) thumbing a lift;
(c) hands about to receive or give;
(d) index finger to lips (shh);
(e) blowing a kiss.

Give the group time to rehearse and then watch all their efforts. A short scene will be sufficient – just a couple of minutes. It's physical expressiveness that you're looking for. By this time they will have more confidence in the power of gesture.

7 Movement work for large groups

● Age range: 11–12 ● Key words: physical control, concentration, suspension of disbelief

You are dancing on the earth . . . you are dancing on the moon . . . You are breathing normally . . . You are breathing in a space suit . . . You are a balloon being blown up . . . you are now a fully blown-up balloon . . . you are very slowly losing air . . . you are a balloon being blown up again. When I clap my hands, you burst (clap) . . . You are another balloon being blown up . . . getting bigger and bigger . . . When I clap my hands the person blowing you up accidentally lets you go (clap) . . .

You are a moth travelling towards the light . . . you are drawn again and again to the same point . . . Now do it in slow motion . . . Now you are a fly buzzing around some food . . . make a fly sound . . . When I clap my hands someone comes along and squashes you (clap) . . .

Now you are a statue. Stand quite still in the pose of your choice. You are completely still . . . very slowly . . . very slowly you are beginning to come to life . . . you can move but only in slow motion . . .

Now let's concentrate on the face . . . move your face in as many directions as possible but don't touch it with your hands . . . Imagine it's made of rubber . . . give your face a good shake . . . now make as monstrous a face as you can . . . Come on . . . uglier than that! Try to scare your friends . . .

Now we're going to be moving in the dark . . . Imagine the lights have gone out and it's pitch black. You can't see a thing. Don't panic. Move very, very slowly towards where you think the wall is . . . No, don't use the real wall of the studio, mime your own wall . . . Now feel along your wall with your hands searching for the light switch . . . you find it and flick it on. Nothing happens. It's still pitch black. Now in mime and still in the dark continue searching until you solve the problem. Just smile and sit down on the floor when you have succeeded.

TEACHER'S NOTES

1. The above order of movement exercise does not have to be followed slavishly. Select and adapt according to your own particular group and situation. The sequence is intended to be progressive but not all pupils will respond in the same way to stimuli. Be flexible and spend longer on what they enjoy.

2. Now ask them to get into pairs. One of each pair is a formless ball of plasticine or putty. The other with his/her hands makes a shape out of the partner.

   Try suggesting: an old person; a soldier; a teacher; a dog; an insect; a monkey; a hatstand; a teapot; a tree. You can add more under the categories of people, animals and objects. At the end they must form a shape which the teacher must guess.

Further development

1. Pupils should mime a scenario (adapted from Jean-Louis Barrault's film *Les Enfants du Paradis*): a young girl is falsely accused of stealing a watch from a very smart gentleman at a fairground. A bystander saw exactly what happened but is dumb: he does not have the power of speech. He has to enact the scene in mime in order to prove the young girl's innocence to the police.

   The mime begins with a fairground where there is lots of bustle and activity. The bystander is at one side watching a Punch and Judy show. The pretty young girl enters and stands watching the show.

   In comes a rather fat, pompous old gentleman with a big gold watch hanging from his waistcoat and he stands beside the young girl. He takes the watch out, corrects the time and puts it back in his pocket.

   In comes the thief who stands beside the fat gentleman, slips his hand behind his back, takes out the watch from his pocket and disappears.

   Now the fat gentleman feels for his watch again, does a double take on realizing it's not there, looks at the young girl beside him, accuses her of stealing his watch, grabs her by the wrist and calls for a policeman.

   A policeman enters. The fat gentleman explains he's been robbed, the girl protests her innocence, the fat gentleman insists it was her and the policeman takes her away to appear in court.

2. This brilliant mime sequence devised by Jean-Louis Barrault is described above as solo work, i.e. for one person miming all the parts (a mammoth task for 12-year-olds, so why not give it to your GCSE group?) but it could also be a group effort. Photocopy the sequence and give it to the groups, allowing them to rehearse before showing the results of their labours.

Divide the class into groups of four – girl, fat gentleman, thief, policeman – and ask them to learn the whole mime sequence by heart putting in as much detail as possible.

The teacher should explain the meaning of double take and show examples to the class. In fact, much depends on the teacher's ability to demonstrate isolated extracts from the sequence, not exactly to show pupils how it should be done, but to give them confidence in the power of speaking without words.

Similar mime sequences can be suggested with the thief:

at a football match;
at a fashion show;
at the cinema;
at the supermarket;
in assembly;
at a tennis match.

If pupils experience difficulty in miming long sequences, ask them to use dialogue to begin with and then, when they're more assured with their story, ask them to express it silently.

8 Starting from sound

- Age range: 11–13
- Key words: vocal freedom, working as a unit

Spread out, don't bunch up. We're going to work in isolation, but together. You've really got to help each other and concentrate on what we are about to do.

We're going to make sounds together, expressive sounds. When I say 'cut' I want the sound to be switched off immediately. Are you ready? . . .

OK, everybody making shushing sounds . . . shhh . . . now whispering . . . hissing . . . mumbling . . . grumbling . . . groaning . . . praying . . . chattering . . . muttering . . . roaring . . . shouting . . . CUT! . . .

Now we'll work backwards . . . shouting . . . roaring . . . muttering . . . chattering . . . praying . . . groaning . . . grumbling . . . mumbling . . . hissing . . . whispering . . . shhh . . . CUT!

TEACHER'S NOTES

1. The important thing to stress is that words are not to be used, only sounds. Also, everybody must attempt to keep together in intensity of sound and volume. To get the class working as a whole with this type of work is difficult, but rewarding if there is a sufficiently high level of concentration.

2. The idea is to develop a group 'feel', a desire to help each other to achieve the required sound as realistically as possible. If there are 'individualists' in the class who wish to stand out by making inappropriate or unnecessarily loud sounds, get the worst offender to be a kind of 'volume button figure' at the front of the class. You can say, 'Karen (Tom) is going to to raise her hand if she wants the sound to go up in volume and bring her hand down if she wants the sound to die down'. The teacher can also serve this function to begin with.

3. This kind of 'chorus' work is essential in drama for getting pupils used to the idea of listening to each other and working together in co-operation, which is, after all, the main purpose of drama.

4. A handclap can be used instead of the word 'cut'.

5. The following can be tried either on the whole class or on groups of five, depending on the amount of concentration generated. Ask the pupils to try to make up a sound to express:

scared of; laughing at; thrilled by; enthusiastic at; bored by; thankful for; keen to; sad at; happy to.

Further development

1. Pupils should form a circle. They are to imagine they are one big, enormous humming top.

They are not to move round in a circle. They move so fast that the only movement visible is the circle getting smaller and larger. At the same time they are humming.

They should work together and 'feel' when the group is going to move inwards and when outwards. The circle shape must be kept. Each person should be very aware of everybody else in the group.

As they move inwards the humming gets softer; as they move outwards the humming gets louder – but there should be no shouting.

Then ask them to form the shape of an enormous mouth. This exercise is called 'Big mouth'. The group should decide who's going to be the lips, teeth and tongue.

The mouth should breathe gently in and out. Ask the group to get into a breathing rhythm and a moving rhythm. They should all work together and help each other. Then tell them the mouth is:

talking; shouting angrily; snoring; blowing; nagging; sighing; shrieking in pain.

'Big mouth' probably works best in groups of five or six rather than the whole class. Make sure that the groups are actually making sounds and not words when given a stimulus like 'nagging'. What we're after are 'nagging sounds', 'shouting angrily sounds', etc.

2. Now get the class into groups of three and give out a photocopy of the following Aesop fable to each group. The instruction is that each group must act out this story entirely in sound. There must be no words used at all.

THE TRAVELLERS AND THE BEAR

Two friends were travelling on the same road together, when they met with a bear. The one, in great fear, without a thought of his companion, climbed up into a tree and hid himself. The other, seeing that he had no chance, single-handed, against the bear, had nothing left but to throw himself on the ground and pretend to be dead; for he had heard that a bear will never touch a dead body. As he lay thus, the bear came up to his head, muffling and snuffling at his nose and ears and heart, but the man immovably held his breath and the beast, supposing him to be dead, walked away. When the bear was fairly out of sight, his companion came down out of the tree and asked what it was that the bear had whispered to him, 'For', he said, 'I observed he put his mouth very close to your ear'. 'Why', replied the other, 'it was no great secret. He only bade me have a care how I kept company with those who, when they get into a difficulty, leave their friends in the lurch'.

9 Moving statues

• Age range: 11–16
• Key word: physical spontaneity

We're going to try freezing in different positions, like statues. When I clap my hands I want you to freeze suddenly in any position you like. Each time I clap my hands you must change your position and the shape of your body. Make the change very dramatic. Ready?

. . . Good, but make the next series of changes even more dramatic. Use your arms, your elbows, your hands, your knees . . . Try to make each position totally different from the last. Use your eyes. The expression on your face must change too.

. . . OK, now when I clap you're going to move just arms and hands as dramatically as possible . . . Now just one arm . . . Now change just the expression of your face each time I clap. Don't touch your face. The face can move without your touching it . . .

Now each time I clap I want you to move just head and neck. Keep looking in as many different directions as you can think of . . .

Now back to moving the whole body again. Don't forget the parts that bend, like wrists, elbows, knees. Ready? . . . Good.

Now when I clap I want you to continue changing dramatically but I might call 'action' after one of the claps. This means that you must change out of your frozen statue state and come to life. Let the body think. Let the position of your body decide what to do. If you're bending down you might be digging the garden or if you've got your arms above your head you might be involved in a 'hold up' at a bank. Don't think of a final position to get yourself into. Keep changing dramatically on each clap and let the body choose what to do. Let the body do the work. When I finally call action you might be in a very awkward position but try nevertheless to 'come to life' as a character . . .

So far we have not used speech. Now on 'action' I want you not only to come to life but to speak as that character. No need to address anybody in the room. Talk to an imaginary person. Again let the body decide the movement. Don't think of a character. Let the position you are in decide the character. If you have faith you'll be surprised how your body will naturally select a suitable character depending on the position you're in. If nothing happens, remain frozen until you're inspired!

TEACHER'S NOTES

1. The teacher may prefer to say 'change' instead of clapping or possibly use a small drum or any instrument which makes a sharp sound.

2. Don't follow a regular rhythm when you're calling the changes, otherwise the pupils will know when the 'action' line is coming and will prepare a character mentally. This is not the purpose of the exercise. The purpose is to make the body itself think spontaneously from its given position. The physical posture itself chooses a character.

3. Try as far as possible to restrain pupils from talking to each other. They must talk either to themselves or to an imaginary character. Say, 'You'll be talking to each other soon enough but not yet'.

Further development

1. The teacher can now ask if anybody would like to go into the middle of the hall or studio. Everybody else stands or sits around the sides. The person in the middle is made to go through a series of changes as above.

When the teacher sees an interesting posture he or she can say 'statue', which means that the person must remain frozen in that position until somebody in the class goes up and begins a verbal improvisation with them, inspired by the physical stance of the 'frozen' person. For example, the position might look like somebody digging. The person going in can say, 'I told you to dig over there not over here. You've ruined my best bulbs'.

What the second person must try not to say is 'What are you doing?' This would put the onus on the 'frozen' person. The onus is on the person going in to give a starting line which can lead to an improvisation. The 'frozen' person responds and the conversation continues until the teacher says 'cut'.

Allow each dialogue to continue until it loses its impetus. Don't let it go on for too long if the pupils are struggling. It's not a question of getting it right or wrong, it's a matter of imaginative flow. Sometimes things flow well and other times they don't but stress that there's no need to get anxious about it.

2. If things are not going well with the whole class watching, do the following:
Ask them each to find a partner and practise giving 'change' commands

to each other until one of them starts something off. Let them rehearse in private. You could suggest that each partner has five 'goes' at calling 'change'. If they haven't thought of a starting line after five 'changes' then it's the other person's turn to have a go.

3. If you are using the whole class it is helpful to have a chair for leaning or sitting. This creates variety of posture and may lead to more ideas for starting lines. For example, someone might be sitting with their hand up and the obvious line to go in with would be, 'Yes, boy (girl), what have you got your hand up for? You want to ask me a question, you want to go to the toilet, what is it? So the person going in is a teacher and the 'frozen' person automatically becomes a pupil.

4. If you find that pupils are still asking, 'What are you doing?', say to them, 'You must qualify that with a further statement. For example "What are you doing? Smoking in the toilets again?" or "What are you doing? Put your coats back on, it's not time to go home yet".'

5. For older pupils and GCSE groups I'd also recommend having two people in the middle 'changing' and a third person coming in. This is much more difficult, as the person coming in has to interpret two physical postures and think of a starting line, but it works very well in threes when the flow gets going and it also makes the improvisations longer.

10 Crowd work

• Age range: 14–16
• Key words: working together, being an individual

They say when you are a part of a crowd you lose your identity. We're going to try being different types of crowds. I'm going to call out various types of crowd or location and I want you to blend together into the kind of crowd my words suggest.

Let's see the kind of sounds and atmosphere that we can create. Be a part of the crowd. Work together. Become one mass, one being. Be alert to what is going on. Ready?

An anti-nuclear protest rally;
A crowd worshipping;
Waiting for a film star to arrive;
Waiting for the train;
A cinema audience watching a horror film;
The House of Commons;
A tennis match at Wimbledon;
Reporters waiting for the Prime Minister;
Cheering the final furlong of the Grand National;
A crowd being addressed by a trade unionist;
A crowd being addressed by Jesus;
A crowd waiting to be executed;
A crowd picketing outside a factory;
A crowd celebrating the New Year;
A crowd watching somebody about to jump from a window ledge.

TEACHER'S NOTES

If any of the above stimuli works particularly well, i.e. if the pupils respond positively and manage to create a realistic atmosphere, then don't necessarily go on to the next one. Stop and work on the one that they respond to. Or go back to the one that they respond to best at the end. You can work as follows:

1. Select a focal point for the crowd to concentrate on, i.e. choose someone in the class to be either the trade unionist or Jesus or the suicide or the Prime Minister, etc.

2. Begin to work on making certain members of the crowd more individual. Ask them to think up an identity – name?, age?, job?, outlook?, married?, children?, etc. Work on the background of some members of the crowd and the reasons for their being there. The individuals in the crowd should speak with greater variety and subtlety.

3. The rest of the crowd can all be given one line to chant or just a few lines to repeat but with no variation, purely repetitive.

4. One of the crowd should be selected to be 'anti' whatever is going on. Another member of the crowd should be fanatically supportive.

5. Working in this way, greater depth in group work can be achieved and the students become more conscious of each other's role-play motivations. We are also trying to make them stand out of the 'crowd fever' to a certain extent and be aware of what is going on around them.

6. If a class is too big, then divide it into two for this kind of work. Some pupils will naturally take the lead in crowd work. Others will be sheep and let someone else do all the work. It's an interesting method of getting to know your pupils.

Further development

1. For the sake of argument, let's say that a crowd watching somebody about to jump from a window ledge works particularly well. Here's a suggested scenario for a filmic approach to the theme:

Scene 1
Suicide writing a letter;

Scene 2
Flashback to the cause of whatever led to the desire to end his/her life;

Scene 3
Friends, relations, family talking at the funeral and arguing about what led to suicide;

Scene 4
Doctors coldly analysing the dead body and the cause of death;

Scene 5
Neighbours being interviewed about the suicide by TV reporters;

Scene 6
The suicide reading his/her letter out loud;

Scene 7
The crowd passing outside the window looks up and sees . . . ;

Scene 8
Suicide jumping.

This scenario works very well for groups of six people.

2. Divide the class into groups of six and ask them to choose whichever crowd location they like best and to work on one of the following themes:

'Being different from the crowd';
'Realising I don't fit in';
'I was swept along by my mates'.

11 Dramatic pause

- Age range: 14–16
- Key words: performance skills, self-discipline

When something dramatic happens in real life or in plays or films, quite often there is a sudden silence just before or just after the event or action.

For example, imagine announcing to your strictest teacher, 'I haven't done my homework'. And I'm sure you've seen many times in Westerns when silence falls on the arrival of an important character in the saloon bar – the piano player stops, the bartender stops washing glasses, the card players stop, people stop in mid-drink and there is dead silence as the camera pans up to . . . 'whoever' . . .

Playwrights employ dramatic pause as a technique for focusing the audience's attention. And it's a technique that can make our improvisations and our scripted work more interesting. So, let's try to create a dramatic pause together.

First, I want you all to say 'no' together and then keep completely quiet. It's more difficult than you think. You have to watch everyone in the class. Ready? Go!

Now imagine that you're all going to be crushed by a falling rock and you shout out 'no!' The rock is falling . . . now!

OK, now let's imagine you're teachers and you see someone outside school who shouldn't be there. You all shout 'Stop' together. Ready? You must leave a pause afterwards, that means dead silence so that you could even hear a pin drop.

Now try for a pause after the following words:

Hey!;   Go!;
Reach!;   Kill!;
You!;   Help!.

TEACHER'S NOTES

1. If it's too difficult to achieve complete silence with a large group, split

them up into groups of four, but it is much more dramatic if the whole class can work together, even for just one or two words plus pause. Some pupils may laugh in the pause through embarrassment. This is natural. Try to understand but be firm. Even succeeding once will give them the idea of what dramatic pause should sound and feel like. If necessary, do something dramatic yourself and freeze them in their tracks. Then say, 'That was dramatic pause'.

2. Ask them to think up and rehearse some dramatic moments in groups. Here are some ideas to get them started:

   (a) You are sitting in an examination. There is complete silence. Suddenly the silence is shattered by a sound (made by one member of the group) outside;
   (b) You cannot stop hiccupping during an examination and your Head is invigilating;
   (c) You are sitting quietly at home reading. Suddenly the silence is broken by the rhythmic beat of a hi-fi from next door;
   (d) You are in the staff room of a school having a cup of tea. There is total silence until the sound of noisy youngsters' voices echoes down the corridor.

3. The above stimuli start from silence and move to sound. Here are some stimuli that start from sound and go to silence:

   (a) You are a group of bullies laughing at a poor little wimp. Suddenly the wimp's big brother appears;
   (b) There is an eerie hum. You are out in the fields walking back home from the pub (or walking down a silent street in a city). You stop. The sound stops. You walk on. The sound starts. You stop. The sound stops, etc. What is it?;
   (c) You are singing your favourite song loudly in class. Suddenly your strictest teacher walks in;
   (d) You hear a fly buzzing in a library. You thump it with a newspaper (or a book) and there is silence. You continue reading. Suddenly the buzzing starts again. After several attempts you finally squash it, but there are some very fierce glares from the librarians.

4. The important thing is not so much the story as the ability to create silence in a dramatic way. This technique will be a useful skill for GCSE performance work or prepared improvisations.

Further development

1. The whole class can work on the following scenario or they can divide into two groups and rehearse separately.

   The title is 'Incident at the OK Saloon'. The setting is the Wild West of America. The characters can include any or all of the following:

gunslinger;	piano player;
sheriff;	singers and hostesses;
undertaker;	girl who loves the gunslinger;
bartender;	old timers;
gamblers;	young bounty hunter.

   There is only one scene. All the characters in the saloon are going about their activities. The doors open and the gunslinger walks in. Slowly, people realise who it is and a silence falls. The gunslinger walks up to the bar, asks for a whisky. The bartender is frightened, looks towards the sheriff. The sheriff nods. The gunslinger gets his drink, drinks it and without taking his eyes off anybody walks out backwards through the door, daring anybody to follow. Sudden relief as the noise surges back in the saloon.

   The above could easily be built up as a very effective piece with much inventiveness and detail from the groups.

2. Here is another scenario which I call 'The Interval'. This one goes from silence to sound to silence. It's an exercise in group concentration. Everybody must be very conscious of each other.

   The idea is to try to create the atmosphere of a theatre bar during the interval. We start from total silence then we hear distant applause followed by murmuring. The murmuring gets louder as the crowd approach the theatre bar – excited chatter, people ordering drinks, laughter, etc. Bar attendants work like fiends to serve everybody.

   Here are some roles the pupils can adopt:

   critics;
   typical theatregoers;
   actors and actresses (not in this play, of course);
   family that doesn't normally go to the theatre;
   couple of snobs;
   VIP in disguise;
   couple of Yuppies;
   programme seller;
   theatre manager.

After a while the teacher rings a bell (or one of the pupils can call 'the performance is about to restart, ladies and gentlemen'.) Still very conscious of each other, everybody finishes drinks quickly and files back into the theatre, the murmuring fading into the distance to total silence.

Place two chairs to serve as the entrance to the bar. That is the route everybody must use. Allot and discuss characters, talk about their respective functions and begin rehearsing. Nobody must come in through a wall.

As they get used to the structure of the piece (silence–sound–silence) give them little snippets of dialogue to use, overlapping so that we hear certain key words only, i.e. 'wonderful show . . .', 'dreadful, not as good as that one we saw last year . . .', 'can't stand that actress . . .', 'drink? . . .', 'gin, dear? . . .'

A dramatic pause can then be put in, perhaps when someone in the theatre bar exclaims loudly, 'God, the people here are a load of snobs!'

3. Another dramatic pause scenario is entitled 'Smoking in the toilets'. This works particularly well.

A teacher suddenly enters the school toilets where smoking has been taking place. The offenders stub out their cigarettes in panic and perhaps accuse the most innocent member of the group.

The characters here can be just ordinary school types.

4. Suggested further reading: *Unman, Wittering and Zigo* by Giles Cooper (Macmillan Education), especially Scene 3; *The Birthday Party* by Harold Pinter (Methuen), especially Act 2, the dialogue interrogation between Goldberg, McAnn and Stanley.

12 Telephone work

- Age range: 13–16
- Key words: self-confidence, spontaneity, verbal articulation, projection

We've got to learn to think quickly in drama, we must have our wits about us. This is called spontaneity. You are given very little or no time for preparation – as in life.

Before going on to telephone work, which is what I want to do today, I want us to sharpen our responses by playing a couple of games in which you have to be very quick-witted.

Get into a circle. I am in the middle of the circle and I want you each to imagine that you are a radio station. Think quickly about what is being broadcast on your station – a pop song, a debate, a play, an interview, the news or whatever.

When I point to you, it means I have tuned in to your station. I want to hear what is being broadcast. If I move on and point to someone else, you switch off and I hear the next person's station and so on.

Don't speak or make a sound unless my finger points at you. I might pass through your station as I'm pointing, in which case you might offer a little snippet of what's going on, but you must stop as soon as I've moved on. Be alert because I might come back to your station. Good.

Now I want to go on to a similar game called 'Reporting from'. Here you're going to be news reporters reporting from a particular location. When I point at you, you start off by announcing 'This is . . . reporting from . . . and the news is that . . . You continue speaking until I point to someone else . . . Ready? Let's go.

TEACHER'S NOTES

1. If you think your pupils can't cope with these exercises straight away, let the class practise what they're going to say or let them think for a few seconds first before launching into them. But don't give them too long to think, otherwise the purpose of the exercise – to get them to work spontaneously – will be missed.

2. Either of these two exercises can also be used independently at any part of a lesson. I say 'game' to the pupils, not 'exercise'. There's no reason why you can't use these 'games' with 11 and 12-year-olds. I have put them in here simply because they are useful to release the verbal juices in preparation for telephone work.

3. If you think that certain pupils might be tongue-tied, you can add, 'Should any of you not be able to think of something, just make a discontinued sound as if your station is off the air' . . . or say something like 'We can't get through to our reporter in Zimbabwe'. Try not to leave pupils feeling embarrassed. If they're obviously struggling, move quickly on to someone else. It's important to stress that, having chosen a news item or a location report, a pupil sticks to the same one and develops it if the teacher comes back to him/her.

4. I find that pupils like to be the pointer in the middle of the circle after a while. There is no reason why they shouldn't be, but let them see you do it first.

5. Here are some suggested starting-off phrases to get them going if they really can't think of anything:

Radio stations
(a) 'Here is the news';
(b) 'Tonight in the studio we have. . .';
(c) 'You dirty rat, you've got me';
(d) 'And that was David Bowie singing . . . Now we have. . .';
(e) 'Here is the weather forecast for Britain and Northern Ireland . . .';
(f) 'I'm phoning to say that people who have long hair should be shot';
(g) 'The soil should be thoroughly dug over' (gardening programme);
(h) 'I've got you under my skin. . .' (singing);
(i) 'God save our gracious Queen. . .' (singing).

'Reporting from . . .'
(a) the Old Bailey at the trial of . . .;
(b) the royal film première . . .;
(c) the council toilets where complaints have been made about . . .;
(d) the shopping centre where I'm speaking to shoppers about a new . . .;
(e) the beauty contest at Olympia where the girls are lining up . . .;
(f) Beirut where today the American Embassy was . . .;
(g) London Zoo where the giant panda is . . .;
(h) Cornwall where the floods have devastated . . .;
(i) Moscow at the summit meeting between . . .;

(j) Transylvania where the legend of Count Dracula has become a reality . . .;

(k) Loch Ness, where once again the monster was spotted . . .;

(l) the top of Big Ben where I'm doing a project on vertigo . . . .

6. After a couple of rounds of 'Radio stations' and ' "Reporting from . . ." ' go on to 'Telephone operator'.

> Telephone operator
> Arrange your chairs in a semi-circle around me. I am a telephone operator and I can tap into as many phone calls as I wish. You are all callers and are phoning somebody either from a public phone box or from home.
>
> You have already dialled the number and are in mid-conversation. If I point to you, I have tapped into your conversation. If I point at someone else, I want to hear what that person is saying.
>
> You can mime speaking until I point to you. Then you must speak immediately.

TEACHER'S NOTES

1. 'Telephone operator' is similar to the two previous exercises but serves to introduce the idea of telephones and personal communication. A telephone is an instrument of great dramatic impact in the theatre. Ask the pupils if they can think of a play (or film) in which a telephone has an important role in the action.

2. For GCSE pupils you could discuss the final scene of An Inspector Calls, by J.B. Priestley, where the phone rings to announce the inspector's arrival yet the inspector has been with the family all evening. Or has he? In this instance the telephone serves to deepen the mystery surrounding the death of Eva Smith. In Jean Cocteau's play, The Human Voice, a woman is on the phone throughout the entire play to the lover who has left her. In the final moments she strangles herself with the telephone cord. In Alfred Hitchcock's film, Dial M for Murder, the setting of a murderous attack on the heroine is whilst she is on the telephone.

3. If you have a stock of telephones with bells in the drama department they will be invaluable here.

   Ask the class to get into pairs and select a telephone card. On each card you will have typed out some suggestions for telephone conversations between two characters. Here are some examples:

- A bank manager phones the police about a break-in at the bank;
- You phone a friend to go out with you;
- You phone a travel agent to book a holiday;
- You phone to make an appointment with a hairdresser;
- You are passing on a juicy bit of gossip;
- You are phoning in reply to an advert for a job in the newspaper;
- Your child comes home from school crying, saying he or she has been bullied. You phone the headteacher;
- Your bank manager phones you about your overdraft;
- You ring up your boyfriend/girlfriend to say you want to end your relationship;
- You are an old-age pensioner who has lost her/his dog. You phone up the police;
- You are an actor/actress who has just been offered the leading part in a major film. You phone a friend who is jealous of your success;
- You phone the police about an all-night party that's on next door;
- You have sighted a UFO. You phone a friend who is sceptical;
- A headteacher phones the parent of a boy or girl who has done something very serious at school. The parent does not believe it;
- You are a worried parent whose child has not come back from school. You phone the school;
- You live above a clothes shop where they always play pop music. You are trying to study for your exams. You phone up the manager;
- You are an old-age pensioner and have lost your teeth. You phone your dentist for a new set;
- A burglar alarm has gone off in your road and you see some boys climbing over a wall opposite. You phone the police;
- You have seen your wife/husband with another man/woman and you decide to ring up a detective agency to have her/him followed;
- You are in communication with an astronaut in a spaceship. He is describing the view of planet earth from the ship.

4. Ask also for a follow-up telephone conversation where the other party phones to continue the situation.

5. Invent more telephone card situations and add them to your stock.

Further development

1. Ask the class to split into groups of four. One of them is in charge of either:

   a busy theatrical agency;
   a hectic newspaper editor's office;
   a major travel agency.

   Ideally, there will be three 'ringing' phones on a desk. The person staffing the phones is on his/her own today. The rest of the staff are off sick. The person at the desk is plagued by ringing phones and must cope as best he/she can. Being very dedicated to his/her job, he/she answers all calls and tries not to panic.

   The people phoning in must have definite requests and insist on prompt action. The person at the desk must be unflustered and not put the phone down or ask to be rung back. The problems must be dealt with at the time, even if he/she is speaking to three different people simultaneously.

   Try one round of three people only phoning up. Then ask them to keep phoning back as different people trying to unsettle the poor, harassed worker.

   N.B.   If there are no ringing phones, it's amazing what mime and a few pupil-based sound effects will do. No props are essential, only imagination.

2. The whole group or GCSE set can work on the idea of a radio phone-in. Choose the biggest extrovert in the class to be the disc jockey, and everybody else takes turns in phoning up with their point of view on the following themes:

   (a) A woman's place is in the home;
   (b) The colour of your skin dictates the job you get;
   (c) God does not exist.

   The disc jockey runs the whole show so he/she must be articulate and imaginative for this to work. Also, make a rule about the number of people who can speak at any one time, e.g. no more than two people can be heard by the disc jockey at any one time. If the disc jockey cuts someone off, then there's nothing they can do about it. The disc jockey chooses which phone calls to accept.

3. Groups of five or more can build up a series of connected phone calls which ought to be scripted and structured to form a complete whole. Themes can be chosen from the following ideas:

(a) Someone's death. A group of relatives phone each other up with the news of someone's death. The telephone conversations reveal the attitude of each member of the family to the person who has died;

(b) A wedding. A group of people who are invited to a wedding party phone each other up and discuss the couple and whether or not they are suited;

(c) Job dismissal. Someone is dismissed from his/her job, and a group of people who work at the same place phone each other up to discuss the fairness or unfairness of the dismissal;

(d) *This is Your Life*. Someone has been asked to appear on the television programme *This is Your Life*, and a group of researchers from the television company phone up some of the people they wish to take part in the show – secretly, of course.

N.B. *This is Your Life* works very well as a set piece in ordinary improvisation sessions. Everybody knows the format and it's excellent for character work.

13 Gibberish

- Age range: 14–16
- Key words: thinking, communicating, vulnerability, listening

We're going to talk a lot of rubbish today. You often accuse each other of talking rubbish, but what do you mean? You don't agree with someone or you don't understand them. Perhaps you don't listen carefully enough or don't want to listen.

When people speak a foreign language it doesn't mean anything to you unless you understand that language. It sounds like a lot of nonsense, but it makes sense to the person who speaks and understands it. We're going to lean to speak 'gibberish' which is a series of sounds with vowels and consonants but no recognisable words.

You must not use any English words at all or any foreign language words. But, if you think about what you're saying, the meaning will be clear. For example, we're all going to be weather forecasters on television. Try to explain what the weather is going to be like tomorrow, in gibberish. Think about what you're saying. I'm going to come round and listen to you. If you want, you can use gesture to enforce what you're trying to say. . . . Good.

Now explain how a washing machine works, in gibberish again.

Now explain how you'd make an omelette. This time I'm going to call out 'English' during your gibberish speech. When I do that I shall want you to switch from gibberish to English words, then I might call out 'gibberish' and you are to revert back to gibberish. If you're thinking all the time about what you're saying, there should be a smooth switch-over.

TEACHER'S NOTES

1. It is best to begin by getting the whole class to work on the exercise simultaneously, as some pupils may feel inhibited (at first) about talking 'gibberish' in front of their friends.

2. Go round the class and listen carefully to everyone, ensuring that no 'English' words are being spoken. Listen also for pupils who make repetitive sounds with no variation whatsoever. This means they are being lazy and not thinking. Others will naturally use gesture and mime to

accompany their gibberish speech. This is good and should be encouraged and praised, but ask them to concentrate mainly on what they are saying – the thought.

3. Here are some more objects. Their purpose can be explained in gibberish by pairs of pupils, one continuing where the other leaves off. Watch to see if they are listening to each other:

a food mixer;	a computer;
a dishwasher;	a tennis racket;
a mattress;	a fishing rod;
an extending ladder;	a video recorder;
a drill;	a space suit.

Another test is to ask the pairs to explain an object in gibberish to each other. The partner must guess what it is.

4. Now we can start on some spontaneous improvisation stimuli. Once again pupils can work in pairs. Just give them the situation and get them to start straight away in gibberish. Once again you can call out 'English' and 'gibberish' at will – or just clap your hands if you prefer, or beat the drum:

(a) Calling round to your best friend's house to see if he/she wants to go out;
(b) Stopping somebody at customs to see if he/she has anything to declare;
(c) Ordering a meal in a restaurant;
(d) Meeting an old friend in the supermarket;
(e) Interviewing the Prime Minister;
(f) Arguing about: (i) your neighbour's dog fouling the garden; (ii) your son or daughter smoking; (iii) the filthy state of the house.

Further development

1. You may find that some pupils' gibberish sounds rather foreign in tone – either Japanese-sounding or French-sounding, etc. Use this by setting up a television advert either in pairs or in threes. Ask them now to do a commercial in, for example, Chinese-sounding gibberish. Give them a short time (one minute) for preparation. By all means take their ideas, but here are some suggestions which work rather well:

(a) a soap commercial (Japanese);
(b) shoes (German);
(c) perfume (French);
(d) vodka (Russian);

(e) hamburger (American);
(f) bowler hat and brolly (English);
(g) spaghetti (Italian).

I know these are stereotypes, but young people are confronted with stereotypes every day on television, and can relate to them. By all means let's get away from stereotypes in drama but they are useful as a start and, besides, don't have to be offensive. They can also be fun.

If the class wants to do these commercials in 'English', let them. Perhaps a double performance for each group can be set up. Do the commercial twice – the first time in gibberish, then straight away in English.

2. Pairs again. One person speaks only in English, the other only in gibberish. The 'English' partner starts off and the conversation continues with the 'gibberish' partner carrying the situation forward, but in gibberish. Both must listen very carefully, especially the 'English' partner, so that a continuity of thought and communication can be established. Here are some starting lines for the 'English' partners:

(a) They're an awful team!;
(b) So you've applied for the job of lion tamer with my circus, have you?;
(c) I'm not having your dog in my cinema;
(d) Are you the person who's come along for the modelling job?;
(e) Please take these encyclopaedias away. I don't want to buy them;
(f) Are you saying there's something wrong with my cooking?;
(g) Why haven't you done your homework?;
(h) Where did you say you put my jacket?.

14 Double-glazed window

• Age range: 13–16
• Key words: mime skills, self-confidence, observation

This exercise is called double-glazed window, and it's a pure mime exercise.

We imagine there is a double-glazed window over here. Let's set up something to represent the window. I am inside the house and you are people going past my window asking me for something in mime. I can see you but I can't hear because my double glazing is so good.

No mouthing words. Just indicate with your hands, face, body what you require. It may be a cup of sugar or a ticket to Wembley.

Who's ready to come past my double-glazed window? . . . If I understand you, it means you've expressed your mime skilfully. If not, you must keep miming until I guess what it is you want . . . I can speak. You can't. Anybody want to take my place?

TEACHER'S NOTES

1. A stage window frame would obviously be the best thing to use but a simple chair will do. It's just a question of creating a barrier through which the householder cannot hear.

2. The whole class can be involved at the same time, but only one person should go up to the double-glazed window.

3. I have devised some reasons for going up to the double-glazed window which can be put on cards to give to each pupil as he or she goes up. Jumble up the cards, make them into a fan shape and let each pupil choose one just before his or her turn. Do not give them out to everyone beforehand as they will tell each other what they have got and the purpose of the exercise will be lost.

4. The only clue the person is allowed to give the householder is whether he or she is a neighbour, a friend or a stranger. This is indicated in brackets at the end of each reason.

5. Pupils can take turns in being householder. Five 'goes' each as householder seems to work. Here are some reasons to express in mime:

- There is smoke coming out of your upstairs window. (*neighbour*);
- A slate has fallen from your roof and nearly killed me (*passerby*);
- I've come to read your gas meter. (*stranger*);
- Your cat's got stuck up a tree. (*neighbour*);
- I fell into a dirty puddle and have been sent home from school by my teacher to get changed. (*son/daughter*);
- I've been beaten up by a gang of skinheads. (*son/daughter*);
- Your car is parked across my drive and I can't get out. (*neighbour*);
- I left my packed lunch in the house and haven't got my keys. (*husband/wife*);
- I am a policeman. I have come to ask you to move your car from across your neighbour's drive. (*stranger*);
- I am the milkman. You haven't paid your bill for three months. (*stranger*);
- Can I use your phone? There's been an accident down the road. (*stranger*);
- I am collecting for charity, would you like to contribute? (*stranger*);
- Would you like to buy a set of encyclopædias? (*stranger*);
- I am the postman. I have a large parcel for you. (*stranger*);
- Your dog has got into my garden and made a mess. (*neighbour*);
- Can I borrow a cup of sugar? (*neighbour*);
- The wind has blown a tree down in your garden and it is lying across my fence. (*neighbour*);
- A flying saucer has just landed in the park across the road. (*neighbour*);
- I've come to empty your dustbins. (*stranger*);
- Your son has kicked a ball through my window. (*neighbour*);
- I am an Avon lady trying to sell you perfume. (*stranger*);
- I am an Indian carpet salesperson. (*stranger*);
- I am a bailiff and have a court order to take away all your furniture because you have not paid your debts. Open the door. (*stranger*);
- I am a Japanese tourist and I would like to come into your house to take a photograph of a typical English family. (*stranger*);
- I am a boy scout/guide. Have you got any odd jobs you want done? (*stranger*);
- I am from the Pools. You have 24 score draws and have won a quarter of a million pounds. (*stranger*);
- I am the coal person. Would you like some coal delivered? (*stranger*);
- I am Chinese. I own the new laundry just opened down the road and am trying to get people to bring their laundry to me. (*stranger*);

- I am a freelance hairdresser. Would you like your hair cut? (*stranger*);
- I am a freelance artist. Would you like your portrait done? (*stranger*);
- I am from Thames Television and I'd like to ask if we could use your house for location filming. We're willing to pay you well, of course. (*stranger*);
- I am a double-glazing salesman. Would you like some double glazing installed? (*stranger*);
- Hello, I am the president of the local amateur dramatic society. Can I interest you in joining? (*stranger*);
- Hello, I am the organiser of the local neighbourhood watch. Would you be prepared to patrol the area once a week in order to deter burglaries? (*neighbour*);
- I am your local vicar. Can I interest you in contributing to our church jumble sale? (*stranger*);
- I am a zoo keeper. An alligator has escaped from the zoo. Have you seen it? (*stranger*);
- I am an elderly neighbour. I am blind. I have dropped my most expensive serving dish on the floor. Would you be kind enough to come round and help me pick up the pieces? (*neighbour*);
- Would you like to come out to the cinema? (*friend*);
- I am a friend of your mother. Is she coming out to play bingo tonight? (*friend/stranger*);
- I lent you my best pen in school today and you didn't give it back. (*friend*).

3. Some of the above are quite complex and difficult to express in mime – purposely so. Allow the pupils a while to study the card before expecting them to perform. They can keep the card for reference while miming. The householder can speak as the mime progresses or you can make a ruling about 'no talking until the mime person has finished'. Do not include complex mime cards for classes you think can't handle it. There are plenty to choose from, and the teacher can add cards as the year progresses or the pupils can suggest some for inclusion in future lessons.

Further development

1. In pairs, ask pupils to use one of the reason cards as the starting point for developing an improvisation. They must, however, do it in two ways. The first time as a pure mime; the second time with words.

2. In groups of four or five, pupils choose a reason card and develop the situation to include a few more suitable characters. They can allocate roles themselves. Again they perform first in mime, then in words.

3. This lesson could additionally be used to play 'householder'. This exercise game helps to sharpen verbal spontaneity. Each pupil is given a card and must knock on the door. The householder opens and the person outside the door has to be the character on the card (see character words, pages 69–70). He/she finds a suitable starting line and continues until the teacher says 'cut'. Another pupil knocks on the door as a different character, and so on. A pupil can serve five turns as householder then go on to the end of the queue and be a caller. As each person finishes he/she goes to the end of the queue and takes another card. This works very well, but make sure that you line up the pupils where they can all see what is going on.

4. Another useful exercise mixing mime and speech is to ask each pupil to call at the door in the usual way but to mime all the nouns, e.g. 'Can I use your (mimes "phone")?' The householder joins in the dialogue with the same mixture of mime and speech. This should make pupils aware of what a noun is. If they speak a noun they are out and must go to the back of the queue.

This exercise can also serve as a prepared improvisation. Let the pairs practise first before any presentation takes place. The results are often hilarious.

Finally, try dialogues miming just the verbs, e.g. 'Can I please (mime "ask") you for the money you haven't (mime "paid") me?' Again this can be very useful in English lessons to make pupils conscious of words and structures of sentences.

15 Rotation improvisation

• Age range: 13–16
• Key words: alertness, self-confidence, self-expression

This exercise is called rotation improvisation. In it there are only two people working at any one time and the rest of the class watch while waiting for their turn to come round.

Person A goes to the centre of the room. Person B goes in, starts talking to Person A with a pre-arranged starting line. The dialogue continues until I say 'cut'. Person A goes off to the end of the queue. Person B is now in the centre and Person C comes in with the same pre-arranged starting line. The dialogue continues again until I say 'cut'.

Basically, each person in the class has two turns. Once as the active person (going in, getting started) and once as the passive person (on the receiving end, having to defend himself/herself). Person A has his/her 'positive' go last.

Let's begin. The starting line is 'You've lost my . . . , haven't you, you skunk'. The person going in substitutes the missing word – any word you like. The person in the middle has to cope as best he/she can.

TEACHER'S NOTES

1. This kind of work sharpens pupils' ability to formulate verbal attack and verbal response. It teaches them to express themselves in a wide variety of situations whilst employing words and mental attitudes of attack and self-defence. They are put very much on the spot and must get out of the situation with imagination, ingenuity, craftiness, etc. It encourages self-confidence and self-expression.

2. Introspective pupils respond to this kind of work as they are not required to be 'up front' all the time and it gives them the opportunity to do quite a lot of listening and watching of others. The less able also particularly enjoy this way of working. It doesn't tax academic ability and brings to the surface the sharpness of their tongues.

3. There are no specific guidelines for developing this kind of work further. The dialogues are short, sharp, witty; or halting, boring, monotonous. In the latter case, it is up to the teacher to call 'cut' before any embarrassment sets in. Once the class gets into the rhythm of rotating and each pupil starts thinking what he/she is going to say a mood of disciplined enjoyment and fun accompanies the lesson.

4. Nobody has to say who they are when they go in to the middle; the role will manifest itself as the dialogue proceeds.

5. The teacher must keep a very tight rein on length of dialogue. Don't let it go on too long. Say 'cut' when it's going well rather than waiting until pupils run out of steam. Always thank them.

6. Be very strict about no talking, unless it's their turn. No exchanges of ideas are allowed while pupils are waiting for their turn. Encourage them to listen and react normally. You are also training them to be a good audience. Laugh if something is funny. Do not jeer. Try to get them to do something different from what the previous people have done. If somebody else uses their idea, they'll have to think of something else to say. Here are some starting lines:
   - 'You've lost my . . . haven't you?';
   - 'How many times have I told you never to . . .';
   - 'Where did you get that ridiculous . . . ?';
   - 'Are you new to this . . . ?';
   - 'What are you doing in this . . . ?';
   - 'I've come to register a complaint!';
   - 'Guess who's moved in down the road?';
   - 'Something very funny happened to me on the way . . .';
   - 'Come here, come here!';
   - 'Sit down, I've got something to tell you';
   - 'Congratulations on . . .';
   - 'Welcome to . . .';
   - 'Is this the queue for . . .?';
   - 'Waiter, there's a . . . in my soup';
   - 'What have you done with my . . .?'.

Further development

1. Another way of working is to build up a composite picture of one particular location. For example, you say to the class that each dialogue is going to take place on a bench overlooking the sea with an old folks' home at the bottom of the hill. There is no starting line. Each pupil thinks

up a character associated with the location – either someone from the old folks' home or just someone out for a walk along the cliffs. Reference can be made to previous characters and events, so as to form a link between them all e.g. 'You know that old woman you were talking to earlier on? She's barmy, you know'.

2. Everybody must either be in strict numerical order or you could ask pupils to go in when they have an idea for a character. No more than two characters should be in the middle at any one time. As soon as one character goes off, another can come in.

3. Listening is even more essential with this kind of work – and so is remembering. If somebody says 'It's breakfast time', then that establishes the time of day, etc. You must leave the scene with a suitable line like 'Ah well, I can't sit here chatting all day, I've got to have my bath'.

4. If anyone goes in twice, it must be as the same character.

5. Here are some suitable locations:
   (a) outside a school staff room at break;
   (b) the corner of a street with a disco a few yards away;
   (c) the kitchen of a busy restaurant;
   (d) in the wings of a theatre while a performance is in progress;
   (e) at the gates of heaven or hell.

6. If it goes really well, there's no reason why you can't say, 'Three people are now allowed at any one time' etc., but don't go beyond four, otherwise it becomes messy.

Working in small groups

16 Objects coming to life

- Age range: 11–13
- Key words: imagination, inventiveness

If you watch cartoons on television you'll know that objects come to life. Trees speak, doors grow eyes, tables run, chairs dance.

In drama we can do the same thing – we can give solid objects a shape and a life and a voice. If you look carefully at the furniture in your house, for instance, you might have a big sofa which could have a deep, booming voice or a little chair which could have a tiny, piping voice.

Let's see how imaginative we can be in bringing objects to life. First of all we're going to make object shapes.

Get into groups of four and work together to form the following solid structures with your bodies:

a crane;
a washing machine;
a food mixer;
a steam roller;
a computer;
a hoover;
a slide projector;
an electric saw;
a grandfather clock;
a cuckoo clock;

a teapot;
a coffee percolator;
a steam engine;
a road drill;
a creaking door;
a heart machine;
a tree;
a racing car;
a wheelbarrow;
a steam kettle.

TEACHER'S NOTES

1. An alternative is to start off by getting pupils to work individually before getting them into groups.

2. Ask them to add *sound effects* to their object, though you'll probably find they'll do that anyway.

3. Go round and comment on the shapes they are making. Ensure that each

member of the group is contributing ideas and carrying out functions. Insist on physical and vocal accuracy based on real-life observation of objects. 'I've never seen a teapot like that before', etc.

4. Another useful exercise to get them working together imaginatively on shapes is to ask them to form the shape of a hand and then add:

a hand pointing;
a fist clenched and unclenched;
a hand punching or pulling or pushing;
a traffic policeman's hand stopping traffic and waving it on;
a hand indicating 'come here';
an eye looking left and right.

5. Finally, you could ask the whole class to work together and form the shape of:

a human being;
a spider;
a monster;
an octopus.

Tell them they are going to concentrate on giving objects a voice and a character. They should work in pairs.

Ask what kind of voice they think a mop would have? They should each practise with a partner and imagine they're a couple of straggly, wet mops talking together. The first line could be 'Cor, they've made me work really 'ard today, Bert' . . .

Then they can practise being a pair of antique silver candelabras on top of a piano. The starting line could be: 'Oh, I've been polished so much today I'm positively glowing' . . .

After that they could try an expensive vase and a cheap vase in a shop.

6. As pupils get into the idea of objects speaking with a particular voice, start to emphasize character. 'The objects have to be real and for them to be real they have to have and experience human qualities and emotions – love, fear, pain etc.' Give the following objects as stimuli, and stress the character conflict which will lead to verbal conflict. Remember they must still form the shape of the object as they speak.

(a) A sooty chimney sweep's brush and one that's hardly been used. Starting line: 'Oh, my God, where have you been?'

(b) A solid silver spoon and an ordinary teaspoon. Starting line: 'That silly woman's put me in the wrong drawer. I shouldn't be in here with you.'

(c) A gold Parker pen and a cheap biro. Starting line: 'Keep to your side of the desk, peasant.'

(d) A wet paint brush and a polished antique table. Starting line: 'Get off me, you horrible creature.'

Further development

1. Get the class into groups of six or seven. Ask them to become objects in a handbag. When they've decided on the objects and who is playing the parts, they must hand a list of objects to the teacher.

The objects are all in the handbag to begin with, and start talking about the owner of the handbag and their way of life in the handbag. As soon as the teacher calls an object from the list, that object has to leave the handbag. One imagines it has been taken out by the owner.

The rest of the objects continue speaking until the teacher calls out another object to be taken out of the bag. The first object is put back in and recounts its adventures.

Carry on until all the objects have been taken out at least once. A similar scenario can take place in the following locations:

a bathroom cabinet;
a mantlepiece;
a library shelf;
a shop window.

2. Pair work can take place using the following objects and starting lines as stimuli:

(a) A pair of football boots. Starting line: 'It's Wednesday today. You know what that means';

(b) A pair of shoes. Starting line: 'I bet she/he will go dancing tonight';

(c) Hot and cold taps. Starting line: 'She/he hasn't had a plumber in for years';

(d) Dustpan and brush. Starting line: 'Life's never been the same since that hoover arrived';

(e) Salt and pepper pots. Starting line: 'There's condensation in this kitchen';

(f) Toothbrush and toothpaste. Starting line: 'You haven't lasted long, have you?';

(g) A cannon and a cannon ball. Starting line: 'There's war again tomorrow';
(h) Quill pen and ink. Starting line: 'What's he writing about?'
(i) Two doorknobs. Starting line: 'I wish people would wash their hands in this house'.

Remember to keep them in their object shapes throughout the work.

17 Talking
in sounds

- Age range: 14–16
- Key words: listening, thinking, communicating

There was once a very funny sketch on television where the actors came into a pub, ordered a drink, met some friends, one of them got jealous because his wife was flirting with someone else, a row ensued and everyone was thrown out of the pub.

All this was done without words. It wasn't done with mime but with chicken sounds. Everybody in the sketch behaved and sounded like a chicken, yet the meaning of what they were saying was perfectly clear.

Get into twos, shake hands with your partner as if you've just met after a long absence and start talking normally: 'Hello there, haven't seen you for ages, what have you been up to?' ... Off you go ...

Stop ... Now continue the conversation using the sound 'Ah ben' ... Go!

TEACHER'S NOTES

1. Once they've got the idea and are communicating in the given sound, call out 'English', which means you want them to revert to normal speech. Then call out 'sound', which means you want them to talk in sound language.

   Listen carefully to the transition from normal speech to sound and vice versa because, if they're thinking, there should be a smooth 'takeover'. This is not really the gibberish which I included in a previous lesson. Gibberish is when pupils invent their own language. This work is from a definite 'given' stimulus which I have devised to go with the situation.

2. Here are some other sounds and situations which can be attempted in pairs:

   (a) A doctor and a patient. Sound is 'Hoo haa';
   (b) Two neighbours gossiping. Sound is 'Bla bla';
   (c) A customer ordering in a restaurant. Sound is 'Men men';
   (d) Collecting for charity. Sound is 'Bibidi-bibidoo';

(e) Teacher telling off a pupil for being late, pupil giving excuses. Sound is 'Doo daa';

(f) A parent commenting on a child's school report and the child replying. Sound is 'Bad bad';

(g) Telling a friend about what you did on holiday. Sound is 'Oh ho'.

Further development

1. The situations in each of the above stimuli can be expanded for groups of four or five but still using the same sound. Some preparation time should be allowed for this, and the whole story performed in sound, not words.

(a) A patient comes to see the doctor about his/her son or daughter who is behaving in a peculiar manner. (A reading of *Ernie's Incredible Illucinations* by Alan Ayckbourn could enhance this particular story). An extra character could be the doctor's receptionist or a nurse. (Sound: Hoo haa)

(b) Two neighbours are gossiping over the garden fence about a newcomer who has just moved in down the road and who is supposed to be a bit of a flirt. The newcomer calls round to meet them and tells them that she intends to do 'bed and breakfast'. The two neighbours are outraged – this will lower the tone of the street, etc. An extra character could be a son or daughter or a local shopkeeper. (Sound: Bla bla)

(c) A teacher goes into a restaurant and orders a meal. Two of the teacher's naughtiest pupils see him/her through the window and proceed to embarrass him/her either by making rude signs or by coming in and sitting at the next table. (Sound: Men men)

(d) A grumpy householder is awoken by a smiling charity collector. The householder is a bit of a scrooge and won't give a penny. The charity collector keeps knocking on the door announcing that the householder will be punished by God for his/her stinginess. That night a ghost appears to the householder saying that unless he/she gives some money to charity he/she will die. The next day the householder gives all his/her money to the charity collector. Extra characters could be either another charity collector, a dog or two ghosts. (Sound: Bibidi bibidoo)

(e) A teacher is calling out the register when a latecomer enters. On being asked why she/he is late she/he proceeds to give a whole string of excuses, none of which the teacher believes. Extra characters could be a goody-goody pupil, a headteacher or a caretaker. (Sound: Doo daa)

(f) A school report is given to parents by a boy/girl. Each subject is gone through meticulously, analysed and commented on. Another character could be the brother or sister who is a real swot. (Sound: Bad bad)

(g) Four friends are talking about their holidays: where they went, what they did, who they went with. Each endeavours to convince the others that his/her holiday was the best. (Sound: Oh ho)

18 Talking in different tones

- Age range: 13–16
- Key words: role play, rhythm, alertness

If you really listen to people when they're talking you'll be able to detect a 'tone'. The tone is the way you feel about something or somebody. A doctor may speak in a gentle, sympathetic tone; an army sergeant major may speak in a clipped, barking tone; a teacher may speak in a monotonous, insistent tone, and so on.

These are just examples to give you an idea of 'tone'. Not every doctor is sympathetic, nor every sergeant major aggressive, nor every teacher monotonous. But what is certain is that everybody speaks with a certain tone, depending on their state of mind and the way they feel 'inside'.

Let's have a go at speaking in different tones ourselves to give you some idea of what I mean. Get into pairs. One of you be number one and the other number two. Number one is going to speak to number two as if he or she is shocked at something number two has done. The starting line is: 'I'm shocked at you, I really am.' Go . . .

Now number two, talk to number one in a shocked tone. Go . . .

Now you're going to talk in a loud tone as if you're showing off, trying to make an impression. The starting line is: 'I've just bought that house actually.' Number one first, then number two. Go . . .

TEACHER'S NOTES

1. Another way to get a class talking in different tones is to go straight for stereotype and say, 'How would such and such a person speak? What kind of tone would a priest use? A photographer, a gangster, a dustman, a magician, a professor, a policeman, a country yokel, a robot, a telephonist, a television newscaster, a butler, a film star?' Although this is unashamedly stereotype work, it does get the class started and from there one can progress to more individual work. This is in fact the value of stereotype work – it gets you started.

Pupils can work on their own in this part of the lesson, i.e. as if they're talking to an imaginary person. Then go on to pair work.

2. Listen to the tone of the whole class when they are speaking. There should be a decided change of tone and rhythm as you take them from stimulus to stimulus. If there is not, it means they are not working, not thinking. Stop the lesson and say, 'You're not really trying. I can't hear that shocked tone or that aggressive tone. Exaggerate a little if you must but make a bigger effort.'

This approach usually has the desired effect. Then you can get them into pairs and give them the following stimuli:

(a) Talking as if you're whispering secretly so as not to be heard. Starting line: 'Do you know what I've done?';

(b) Talking as if you're nagging someone. Starting line: 'If I've told you once I've told you a thousand times';

(c) Talking excitedly as if you've just had great news. Starting line: 'Hey, guess what's happened to me';

(d) Talking as if you're consoling somebody. Starting line: 'Never mind, it wasn't your fault, you weren't to blame';

(e) Talking as if you're trying to explain something to somebody who is not very bright. Starting line: 'Look, it works like this, I'll tell you again';

(f) Talking as if you're remembering the old days. Starting line: 'Ah yes, and do you remember the time when we . . .?;

(g) Talking as if you're annoyed with someone. Starting line: 'I'm sure it was you';

(h) Talking as if you're really pleased to see someone. Starting line: 'Hello, how lovely to see you';

(i) Talking as if you're bored but trying to be polite. Starting line: 'Really, how fascinating'.

The *Character words* on pages 69–70 of this book should also provide you with more ideas for character types leading to typical situations you can use as above.

The last stimulus brings me on to the next part of the lesson which is called 'What we say is not what we think'. How often do we actually say what we think? Isn't it true that quite often we say one thing but are thinking another? For example, someone has gone to the trouble of cooking you a very expensive meal but it tastes awful. You don't want to hurt their feelings so you say how nice it is but in fact you are thinking something else.

If we practise this kind of 'double thinking' in drama, it will help to make our role-play and characterisation more true-to-life and give it greater depth. Get into pairs again. I'm going to give each pair a card. On the card is printed the starting line for a dialogue plus a hidden thought for one character. You devise and plan the situation to last for five minutes. Rehearse, practise and prepare. Choose a card.

TEACHER'S NOTES

1. Here are some situations for 'What we say is not what we think'. Transfer them on to cards and use as required. You don't have to give each pair a different one if you don't want to. You could just as easily give them all the same situation if you feel it merits it. In this way the other ideas can be used at some other time! The 'hidden thought' can belong either to one character or to both.

- Starting line: 'It's a pleasure to be working for you'. Hidden thought: 'I hate your guts';
- Starting line: 'It looks as if we'll be sharing the same office'. Hidden thought: 'Fancy my having to have that wimp in my office';
- Starting line: 'How nice to see you after all these years'. Hidden thought: 'Stuck up, affected so and so!';
- Starting line: 'Ah yes, it's Wilkins, isn't it?' Hidden thought: 'Who is this person?';
- Starting line: 'You're looking great today. What shampoo do you use? Hidden thought: 'God, what a mess';
- Starting line: 'That's very kind of you'. Hidden thought: 'I bet she/he is after something';
- Starting line: 'This is delicious'. Hidden thought: She/he can't cook to save her/his life';
- Starting line: 'I'll give you the recipe'. Hidden thought: 'You fat toad!';
- Starting line: 'I'm going to Miami for my holidays'. Hidden thought: 'I'm really going to Bognor but why should I tell him/her?';
- Starting line: 'What a coincidence, fancy meeting you on holiday!' Hidden thought: 'Oh God, what's she/he doing here?';
- Starting line: 'I got dozens of presents for my birthday'. Hidden thought: 'I only got two really';
- Starting line: 'You're such a popular teacher'. Hidden thought: 'Everyone hates you';
- Starting line: 'I think your mother's really nice'. Hidden thought: 'She's an old battleaxe';
- Starting line: 'Your boyfriend/girlfriend is great'. Hidden thought: 'Where did she/he pick him/her up';

- Starting line: 'Where did you get your sweater?' Hidden thought: 'God, it looks awful!';
- Starting line: 'That hat suits you'. Hidden thought: 'It covers your bald spot';
- Starting line: 'I get £10 a week pocket money'. Hidden thought: 'Wish I did, I only get 50p if I'm lucky!';
- Starting line: 'My dad works for IBM'. Hidden thought: 'Actually he's on the dole';
- Starting line: 'You're the best teacher in this school'. Hidden thought: 'I hope you'll give me a good mark';
- Starting line: 'You haven't done too badly this term, Ann/Tony'. Hidden thought: 'You're a bit slow but I don't want to discourage you'.

Some of these stimuli may slow down the pupil's natural responses and may produce some stilted, unsure dialogue (conversely, there may be some interesting examples of dramatic pause!) This is because they are being asked to think their responses and, initially, they may find it difficult. They may be unable to progress the dialogue very far. Again, the effort is the important thing. They're being asked to do two different things at the same time, so we must not expect brilliant, free-flowing, spontaneous dialogue. Young people are not used to checking their responses; they're much more direct than adults so this kind of work may be alien to them. However, this is still a most valid drama technique to master, and will help a great deal in prepared, scripted work and in textual study.

Further development

1. In pairs ask pupils to devise a scene in which:

   (a) neither of them reveals the hidden thought;
   (b) one of them reveals the hidden thought;
   (c) both of them reveal the hidden thought.

   Using *character words* (pages 69–70) you can ask them to build these scenes around a particular character.

2. In pairs, ask them to reveal the hidden thought immediately after the starting line, almost as a direct challenge, e.g. 'Where did you get that sweater? It looks awful!' This leads to an argument.

3. Ask students to develop any one of the following ideas and decide for themselves whether they are going to be direct or whether they are going to skirt round the truth:

(a) A doctor telling someone they have terminal cancer;
(b) An employer telling an employee, after 20 years' faithful service, that regrettably she/he is going to be made redundant;
(c) A builder telling a client that the wall of an old cottage she has just bought collapsed as soon as he/she started work on it;
(d) A teacher telling a very hard-working pupil that he/she has failed an important exam;
(e) A person telling his/her partner (who is in very frail health) that they've won the pools;
(f) A headteacher telling an influential parent/governor that his/her son is going to be expelled from the school;
(g) A young girl telling one or both of her parents that she is pregnant.

4. Suggested further reading:
A Taste of Honey by Shelagh Delaney (Methuen) Act 1 Scene 2; *The Crucible* by Arthur Miller (Heinemann) Act 1 Scenes 1 and 2; *Billy Liar* by Keith Waterhouse and Willis Hall (French) (from Barbara/Billy dialogue to the end of Act 1).

19 Surrealism

• Age range: 15–16
• Key words: intelligence, spontaneity

As we become more proficient in drama, we go on to more demanding stimuli in order to tap our subconscious creative resources.

Surrealism was a literary movement of the early part of the 20th century which centred on the idea of spontaneous writing and the connection between seemingly unrelated objects. For example, I say to you, 'What is the connection between a violin and a piano?' Well, that's simple, they're both musical instruments. But what is the connection between a violin and an egg? Or a piano and lamb chops? You've got to think, haven't you?

What I want you to do is to get into pairs and we'll find out just how good you really are at spontaneous work. I'm going to call out a couple of unrelated objects. I'll give you one minute to formulate a drama and a connection around these objects. Ready?

TEACHER'S NOTES

1. Here is a list of unrelated objects which you can call out. Be very strict about timing. One minute only for discussion. Then pupils must perform.

   (a) a glass eye and a tea strainer;
   (b) a guitar and a newspaper;
   (c) a telephone and a cloud;
   (d) a glove and a diary;
   (e) a knife and after-shave lotion;
   (f) a dog and a cinema;
   (g) a bar of soap and a glass of beer;
   (h) a light bulb and a rose;
   (i) a clock and a banana;
   (j) a typewriter and a football.

   The results of pupils' deliberations don't necessarily have to last long. It's just a question of making the connection between the objects. Short, sharp, witty sketches are what to aim for, but don't dictate the style of presentation. Leave it to them. This exercise does wonders for sharpening spontaneous reactions.

Another aspect of surrealism was an emphasis on dream life. As you know, in films the action usually slows down when there is a dream sequence, or there may be a change of colour, or the screen goes hazy. We can develop various techniques in drama for portraying dream sequences, flashbacks and fantasies in order to make our plays and improvisations more exciting. How would you express a flashback in theatrical terms?

TEACHER'S NOTES

1. Let the pupils make suggestions and let them experiment in groups with flashback techniques. The main point to make is that there must be a change in the rhythm of the narrative flow in order for the audience to be made aware that the action is shifting backwards in time. There is no need to say 'We are going back in time' or presenting a board to the audience with the words 'Five years before' written on it (unless of course you're doing a melodrama or a silent film scenario). All you have to do is 'plant' a line just before the flashback, i.e. 'Do you remember when . . . ? or 'I remember that day as if it were yesterday', followed by a definite pause and a slow-motion movement of the characters, either backwards or turning round on the spot. The audience then knows that something has happened to the time scale. The performers should start the flashback scene at normal speed, pause at the end, do the slow-motion movement and come back to the present time. There is no need for sophisticated lighting to achieve any of this (though it would be nice) but music cued at the right moment would help the effect. (See the 'Trixie and Baba' scenario, pages 91–2). Here are some suggestions and ideas for flashback, dream and fantasy sequences:

   (a) A patient recounts a dream or nightmare to his/her doctor. As the patient speaks we have the dream acted out in mime with the voice of the patient perhaps pre-recorded on tape and played back during the dream itself. Ask each group to write out a dream action sequence as well as perform it;

   (b) A group of old people who used to go to school together are having a reunion. They remember various pranks they used to get up to when they were young. A flashback sequence is required for each episode. It must be made clear in the presentation what is time past and what is time present;

   (c) An employee who over the years has been subjected to much humiliation by his/her ogre of a boss fantasizes about a time when he/

she can reverse roles. Again pupils should concentrate on making a definite distinction between fantasy and reality sequences.

Further development

Text: *Billy Liar* by Keith Waterhouse and Willis Hall.

1. Pupils work on a monologue telephone conversation similar to Billy's speech at the close of Act 1 where he tells his undertaker boss exactly what he thinks of him.

   The speech starts off with one person answering the phone. The call is from someone who evidently has some control over this character and whom this character would dearly love to tell to go to ****. When the telephone conversation ends, the character fantasizes about how he or she would treat this person if possible. Then his/her mother comes into the room and this brings him/her back to reality rather sharply.

   Write the monologue to last for approximately 2 minutes.

2. In pairs pupils work out in dramatic terms a sequence in which Billy goes to London to meet the famous Danny Boon. They should do two versions: one is a fantasy and everything turns out successfully for Billy; and the other is a disaster – Danny Boon has never heard of him, has got no time for him, etc.

3. In pairs pupils work on an improvisation sequence where as usual, Billy is being told off by his father. In the middle of the argument, Billy has a fantasy in which his father grovels at his feet because he's scared of him. The fantasy is brought back to reality by Geoffrey saying, 'Did you hear what I said?'

4. In pairs, pupils improvise a scene similar to the one in which Barbara and Billy are seated on the sofa talking about what married life means to them. The scene must have two fantasy sequences. One is Barbara's view of what married life would be like and the other, Billy's version.

5. In groups of seven, pupils devise a nightmare sequence in which Billy experiences the following dreams:

   (a) His grandmother comes back to haunt him because he treated her so badly;

(b) Rita keeps asking him for her ring;
(c) Barbara has committed suicide because he deserted her;
(d) Arthur is an ugly, toothless degenerate;
(e) His mother and father are celebrating with champagne because Billy has died.

After allocating the various parts and rehearsing, one of the group has to volunteer to script the whole lot.

The scene can begin with Billy falling asleep, move on to the nightmares and end with him waking up with a start.

6. Two pupils read the scene between Billy and Liz in Act 3. They then improvise the scene at the station with Liz waiting for Billy to arrive so they can both go to London. Billy turns up and tells Liz he can't go through with it. She realises his immaturity. The scene ends with Billy going dejectedly back home – as in fact happens in the play.

20 Character words

I have a series of cards here. On each card is printed the name of a particular character, for example, a policeman or a nurse or a boxer. I'm going to call out each character as it comes up in the cards and I want you first of all to mime what you think that character does. Remember, mime – don't speak, at least not yet. OK, ready? . . .

A window cleaner . . . a cook . . . a photographer . . . Good.

Now find a partner and when I call out the character, one of you is the character and the other is someone else connected with that character. Ready? . . .

A doctor . . . you can speak now . . . one of you can be doctor and the other can be a patient. Off you go . . .

Now let's try a . . . traffic warden . . . Go . . .

Character words

GANGSTER	JUDGE	LION TAMER
GOALKEEPER	WATCHMAKER	VENTRILOQUIST
GURU	PROFESSOR	VET
GUARD	DUSTMAN	BOUNCER
BARBER	PLUMBER	AVON LADY
GYPSY	REPORTER	TV NEWSCASTER
SHOEMAKER	GAMBLER	WEATHERMAN
COMEDIAN	TEACHER	BUTLER
TAILOR	GARDENER	THATCHER
SOLDIER	SCIENTIST	SCULPTOR
HIJACKER	SPY	POTTER
PLASTERER	DENTIST	ACROBAT
MASK MAKER	ARTIST	SAILOR
CONDUCTOR	HAIRDRESSER	PETROL ATTENDANT
CONTORTIONIST	ROBOT	HOTEL RECEPTIONIST
NETBALL PLAYER	CLOWN	MOUNTAINEER
COOK	CHEF	KUNG FU EXPERT
CRICKET PLAYER	JOCKEY	JUROR
DETECTIVE	DEVIL	ICE HOCKEY PLAYER

FOOTBALL PLAYER	POSTMAN	KING
EXPLORER	MILKMAN	DOCTOR
SQUASH PLAYER	CARPENTER	PENSIONER
FISHMONGER	TRAMP	BULLY
FORTUNE TELLER	BOXER	AIR STEWARD(ESS)
BASKETBALL PLAYER	DOCKER	POLE VAULTER
FAIRY	HARPIST	SALES ASSISTANT
RUGBY PLAYER	TELEPHONIST	PSYCHIATRIST
CAMERAMAN	PILOT	DRUG ADDICT
TIGHTROPE WALKER	TEA LADY	PRISONER
EXECUTIONER	VIOLINIST	DRUNKARD
PRIEST	WEIGHT LIFTER	MURDERER
PIRATE	AUCTIONEER	BARMAN
COAL MINER	SHELF STACKER	PRIESTESS
TRAPEZE ARTIST	TAXI DRIVER	VICAR
WINDOW CLEANER	SLAVE	BRICKLAYER
ASTRONOMER	MECHANIC	SEAMSTRESS
FLOWER ARRANGER	SURGEON	BARMAID
SNAKE CHARMER	TRAFFIC WARDEN	BISHOP
FILM STAR	THIEF	BARRISTER
JUGGLER	LIEFGUARD	BAILIFF
OPERA SINGER	NURSE	ESTATE AGENT
BURGLAR	UNDERWATER DIVER	TV NEWSREPORTER
SECRETARY	POP SINGER	ACCOUNTANT
BELLRINGER	TAXIDERMIST	SERVANT
MAGICIAN	DIAMOND CUTTER	MAGISTRATE
ELECTRICIAN	CINEMA	BANK MANAGER
NUN	PROJECTIONIST	CHAMBERMAID
MONK	WRESTLER	TENNIS PLAYER
GLASS BLOWER	PIANIST	BASKETBALL PLAYER
PHOTOGRAPHER	ACTOR	PUPPETEER
DANCER	TRUMPETER	CELLIST
ATHLETE	ANGEL	DRUMMER
WAITER	ONION SELLER	POLICE OFFICER
CLEANER	PAINTER	HECKLER
FIREMAN	CHIMNEY SWEEP	

TEACHER'S NOTES

1. There are many ways in which these character words can be used. They are a constant source of ideas and a really useful stimulus both to the pupil and the teacher. The teacher should make up a set of cards with character names on the back of each card.

2. Simply give a card to a pupil who has to mime the word on the card to the rest of the class. The class guess what he or she is miming.

3. Younger pupils like to come out, close their eyes and then point to the character words list. Whatever character word their finger points to is the one they must interpret.

4. For third years and above, I have a more difficult exercise. I give three different cards to a group of three pupils. Each member of the group must adopt a role and in some way work on an improvisation which links the three characters, find a setting, a situation, a story line, some background to the characters' recent and past lives, etc. Five minutes to prepare.

5 With GCSE groups, try groups of four or five choosing different cards and linking the characters. Again this is not easy, so be selective.

6. Character words always seem to work well, perhaps because the pupils know that the teacher does not know what is coming up on the cards. The teacher should be as much in the dark as the pupils and if challenged should do a few spontaneous 'mimes' him/herself. Always stress that you don't know what's coming up. Say, 'You are creating this lesson, not me'.

7. Give each pair a card and tell them they must prepare a television commercial advertising something relevant to that character. The commercial should last 30 seconds. Preparation time depends on the ability of the class, so each drama teacher should rely on their own good practice. You could try this in threes as well as pairs. Don't let the pupils persuade you to change their card if they don't like it for some reason. Say, 'I didn't plan to give it to you. You must accept whatever comes up in drama, like everyone else'.

8. The whole group can work together on this one. Call out a character and point to a person in the class who is to be that character. Everybody in the class must now work towards establishing that character as the focal point of a scene. For example, you might call out 'priestess'. Everyone can make her the worshipping focal point.

Go straight on to another character as soon as they've got the idea. You could suggest a few characters that generally work well for this kind of work such as conductor, cameraman, photographer, teacher, airline pilot, supermarket manager, traffic warden, thief, pop singer, onion seller, lion tamer, petrol attendant, hotel receptionist, king, queen, barman, doctor.

9. Ask the class to get into pairs. Give each pair a card. They must set up an interview situation either for a job or an interview on radio or television. The interviewee is the person on the card; the other person is the interviewer. They can then swop roles. These 'interviews' can be prepared over a 5-minute period before being shown either to the rest of the class or to the teacher as he or she walks round. Here are some examples of what happened in one of my classes (14-year-olds):

(a) *Robot* – pupils devised the situation of a robot interviewing another robot who wanted to go up in the world and be a computer;
(b) *Bellringer* – pupils had a country yokel-type bell-ringer being interviewed by the lady of the manor as part of a radio programme;
(c) *Chambermaid* – a maid was interviewed by a snooty but lascivious hotel manager;
(d) *Tennis player* – an Australian tennis player wanted to be a coach and was interviewed by someone from the British Tennis Association. Prejudice against Australians came up in the course of the improvisation, with some very amusing repartee;
(e) *Hotel receptionist* – interview between the manager and a potential receptionist who was trying to cover up her cockney accent.

Further development

1. In mixed schools the following 'battle of the sexes' character work can be attempted. Choose characters who are usually associated with predominantly male or female work and ask the pupils to work on anti-stereotype improvisations. Groups of four or five are best for this:

(a) *Dustmen* – a group of dustmen go on strike because women are now being allowed to work as dustmen;
(b) *Secretaries* – a group of female secretaries discuss the arrival of the first male secretary in the firm;
(c) *Builders* – a woman goes for a job as a plasterer or a plumber and is ridiculed until she proves that she can do the job as well as any man;
(d) *Sheep shearers* – a group of Australian men are having a sheep-shearing competition when they discover that one of the contestants is a woman.

2. Devise a television discussion programme using groups of three boys and

three girls to talk through the prejudice involved with the following jobs: orchestra conductor, coal miner, fireman, judge, airline pilot, telephonist, taxi driver, lion tamer, chambermaid. There should be a compère, making seven in a group. The theme is: 'Are all jobs open to men and women? Or are some jobs more suitable for men and some more suitable for women? We have in the studio tonight six guests to discuss this rather thorny issue . . .'

3. In groups of four, pupils work on the script of a television news broadcast. Two of them read the text and the other two have to act out all the characters mentioned in the news reports. They should cram in as many different types of characters as possible, e.g. 'Good evening, here is the news. Amongst other things tonight, the Queen's bedroom is invaded by a strange man, the Prime Minister is given a dressing down by a shop floor worker, more drug addicts are crowding our inner-city streets, doctors are threatening to go on strike, as are the British Leyland car workers and lady telephonists in Ramsgate. War in the Middle East with chemicals, and the cricket scores as usual brought to you by . . .'. Then each item should be expanded with greater detail.

21 Family groups

• Age range: 13–14 and 15–16 (further development) • Key word: harmonising

We all belong to some sort of family, whether we like it or not. Our own family at home may be noisy or quiet, friendly or aggressive, rich or poor, but one thing is for certain – the family has a powerful influence on our lives. Mum and Dad, Father and Mother, Mummy and Daddy, Fred and Sybil, 'Oi, you!', or whatever you call them, brothers and sisters, aunts and uncles, the whole brood of endless relatives, even the dog and the budgie – all are a part of our early development and have a greater influence on us than we realise.

At school you gravitate towards certain people and become a gang or a bunch of friends, which is really another form of 'family'. Even the most ardent individualist will have some need for companionship, even if it's for an animal. Remember Kes? The boy's real life family is so awful that he forms a deep attachment to the kestrel which becomes a substitute for his family. We all need love and affection and if we don't find it in our real-life family we seek it consciously or unconsciously elsewhere.

Today in drama, as an experiment, we're going to get into family groups. Look around the room and join the people you feel closest to. No more than six in a group. . . Go on . . . OK.

Now, you've made your choice. Look at your family again and make sure you do like them. If you don't there's still time to change. Change now or it'll be too late. Once we've set the family groups I won't allow you to change. OK? All happy with your family groups? Good.

First of all decide who is going to be mum, dad, brother, etc. and show me a typical family photograph grouping. Imagine the family is having its photo taken and just freeze into whatever pose you think is right . . . and freeze! . . .

OK, now show me the family in action at home one early Monday morning . . . now at Sunday lunch . . . Now there's been a crisis in the family – one of you is ill and the others have to look after you . . . Go!

TEACHER'S NOTES

1. Working in the above manner, fairly spontaneously to begin with, get the groups used to working together as a unit to solve problems. Ensure that each person in the group has a character identity within the family. Experiment with the following stimuli:

   (a) One of you has lost his/her job. How do the others feel about that?
   (b) One of you is going to get married;
   (c) One of you feels unwanted;
   (d) One of you comes into a lot of money;
   (e) One of you is expelled from school.

   Now ask each group to polish one or more of the above stimuli and rehearse the most successful one towards a five- or ten-minute performance.

2. In the same family groups (or they can change now if pupils wish) ask them to choose an improvisation based on two totally opposite types of family. One is called 'The Highbrows'; the other is called 'The Lowbrows'.

   The 'Highbrows' are clever, caring, articulate, read books, the quality press, dress nicely, have money, go to lovely undiscovered areas for their holidays, eat out at restaurants, have a designer kitchen, colour co-ordinated decor, a farmhouse in Tuscany.

   The 'Lowbrows' are – the opposite.

   (a) Ask each group to prepare both improvisations.
   (b) Ask each group to rehearse only one improvisation.
   (c) Ask each group all to act at the same time, but alternately, i.e. one group says a sentence, another group says a sentence, etc. If you can arrange for a highbrow group to meet a lowbrow group, then a highbrow group, etc. the results are very amusing because of the great contrast.

3. Now an improvisation in which an individual is beginning to be quite distinct from the rest of the family, for example, a member of a family who has been abroad, and has not seen the family or lived with them for some time. The family know this special visitor is coming and are making preparations. This person is different from the rest of the family, has grown away from them, does not feel a part of them any longer. Here are some suggestions:

(a) A working-class family whose son/daughter has been away at university;

(b) A middle-class family, who are expecting a visit from a rich uncle who has been away and made his fortune in America. Everything is too 'small' to the American uncle;

(c) A family who are expecting a visit from their son/daughter who has been abroad and married a foreigner without telling them.

Further development

1. For GCSE groups I would recommend the following plays for studying the theme of families before coming on to ideas for written, as well as practical work:

   (a) *Stage Write*, edited by Gervaise Phinn (Unwin Hyman). There are three short plays worth reading here: 'Home' by Berlie Doherty, 'Keep on Running' by Roger Burford Mason and 'Audition' by Alma Cullen;

   (b) *Dear Octopus* by Dodie Smith (French);

   (c) *This Happy Breed* by Noel Coward (French).

2. In groups of four, pupils build up, through improvisation and based on their reading, a piece of theatre on the theme of 'alienation'. Each writes notes on the structure of the piece, his/her character and some of his/her most important dialogue.

3. Pupils write a short extract from a play on the following theme: A teenager's love of gardening, bird-watching or poetry brings him/her into ridicule within the family.

4. Pupils choose one of the following unusual families around whom to build a drama or a comedy:

   (a) An Italian Mafia family whose son/daughter has joined the police force;

   (b) A 'monster' family whose son/daughter has become a monster catcher;

   (c) A gypsy family who are being harassed to leave the plot of land on which they've camped for years.

22 Decision-taking

- Age range: 14–16
- Key words: initiative, active listening, positive helping

Making decisions is an important part of life, therefore in drama we try to set up situations which will test our decision-taking qualities.

Sometimes decisions are made for us but sooner or later we have to face making a choice or taking a particular path and that means having to make a decision. Also we sometimes have to reach a decision as part of a group (if we're sitting on a committee, for example) or we have to make decisions for other people, our families, our friends or those incapable of making decisions for themselves. It's all part of the process of growing up.

We're all going to work very hard at negotiating with each other in role play. We're going to reach a decision in whatever situation I give as a stimulus. Get into groups of five or six. You'll have thirty minutes to discuss, prepare and rehearse.

TEACHER'S NOTES

Choose a suitable theme from the following stimuli, one that you think your particular group will respond to. You can either give them a choice or they can all work on the same theme. I have recommended certain plays as a study aid to various themes. These can be read by the individual group alone or by the whole class if they are all going to work on the same stimulus.

1. A group of assorted pupils and teachers have been accidentally locked in a room by the caretaker. He has now gone home. There is nobody else in school. What happens?

   Suggested reading: *Gotcha* by Barry Keefe (Methuen); *Detention* by David Calcutt (Heinemann).

2. A group of schoolchildren go to see a very strict teacher or headteacher about a series of decisions he/she has made about:
   (a) a school outing to a museum;
   (b) a detention or punishment which he/she has made;
   (c) the wearing of school uniform which will be imposed on a day traditionally set aside for 'wear what you like';
   (d) severe cuts to drama on the timetable.

Suggested reading: *Our Day Out* by Willy Russell (Hutchinson).

3. A family meets to decide any of the following:
   (a) to move house because they can no longer afford to stay in a very expensive area;
   (b) to move house because some foreigners have moved in down the road;
   (c) to have their house painted yellow as a gesture of support for their local football team and because all the rest of the street are going to do so;
   (d) to accept a son or daughter marrying outside the family religion.

   Suggested reading: *Terraces* by Willy Russell (Hutchinson); *Spring and Port Wine* by Bill Naughton (French).

4. A group wish to be considered for a youth initiative scheme. The leader has just given them their first task prior to an interview which will decide what qualities the group will need to show in order to be accepted on the scheme.

   Suggested reading: *Fit for Heroes* by Charlie Moritz (Cambridge University Press).

5. A group of young people sit on the committee of their local youth drama group. The (adult) secretary has asked them to help select a new drama teacher by conducting the interview themselves.

Further development

1. When dealing with prepared work for older groups it is as well to make them aware of the following points regarding characterisation:

   Are they going to play themselves or are they going to be somebody completely different? If so, then they must decide on who the person is – name, age, height, nationality, job, marital status, education, outlook on life, etc. They must read plays to gain a wider knowledge of character and technique. If they are merely going to imitate or mimic another character it would be like a television comedian who paints in broad strokes or exaggerates certain qualities, for example an old man walking with a walking stick or a policeman bending his knees and saying 'ello, ello, ello'. Explain that this is called parody or caricature, that it's good fun and it's a start, but that serious role play stems from concentration and the willingness to be involved.

2. Some young people find it difficult to 'be another person' unless they are

stereotyping or imitating. It's best to encourage them to mimic if they have the ability to do so, but stress that what they are doing is slavish imitation. On the other hand there are those who wish just to be themselves and have no inclination to project themselves into any form of serious role play. Asking them to take on the role of a particular character will produce no result.

3. Serious role play can only work if pupils can identify both with the character and the situation. In other words drama teachers have to move their imagination in order to avoid the constant cry of 'that's boring'. But, at the same time, their lack of wider experience of life and the limiting influences of watching third-rate television programmes condition their responses and make them react with 'that's boring' almost as a defence mechanism. There is no easy solution to this problem. In drama, especially at GCSE level, pupils must learn that to be vulnerable and passive within the group is just as important as being positive and assertive.

4. In order to emphasize the dual factors of positive and negative, aggression and passivity in decision-making situations, ask them to:

   (a) Change roles within their improvisation; be strong if they were weak. How do they feel?;
   (b) Do their improvisation as a comedy caricature and then play it deadly serious. How do they feel different as performers?;
   (c) Say in what way they contributed to any decision-making within the group? Were they a hindrance or a help? Why?;
   (d) Say in what ways drama helps them to make decisions in life;
   (e) Write a short essay on the session, describing their specific role within the group. What did they do to help?

23 Help

- Age range: 14–16
- Key words: alertness, concentration, sensitivity

Sit cross-legged in a big circle. I'm going to give you all a number . . . If I call out your number you are to go to the centre of the circle and await help. I shall then give the stimulus: You are stranded in the middle of the countryside. Your car has broken down and you are waiting for help.

I then call out more numbers and those people have to go into the middle of the circle and offer the appropriate help. Don't go in unless I call out your number. This is spontaneous improvisation. You enter the scene 'in role' and can leave when you like. You adopt a role suitable to the occasion. Keep the dialogue going until I stop you. You can re-enter the scene but only in the same role.

TEACHER'S NOTES

1. Call out numbers to begin with but the aim eventually is to get the pupils to volunteer help. If they volunteer from the beginning that's fine, but make a ruling that there should be no more than four people in the scene at any one time or the focus of attention may become 'messy'.

   Allow the improvisation to continue until such time as help has been given and received (or not given and received).

2. You can learn a lot about your pupils from this exercise. The desire to help may be there with some pupils but the ability to adopt a suitable role quickly may be lacking. This kind of work is really for those who have done quite a lot of spontaneous improvisation as a part of their course. Otherwise you may find that certain GCSE pupils may be 'stumped'. If so, get them to work in smaller groups first before moving into the big circle. Give the stimulus to all the groups and allow them to work at it for a few minutes while you go round observing their efforts.

   If they prefer this way of working, give them a few more stimuli in groups in order to build up their confidence before moving on to big circle work. But remember that being in the big circle is the aim. We are trying to get them to be positive about helping others whatever the situation. But don't judge. 'Fence-sitters' and those who don't want to help also have their place in the scheme of things. Here are some more 'help' stimuli:

(a) You have just dropped a hot frying pan onto the floor in your kitchen;

(b) Your washing machine has just overflowed;

(c) You've just cut your finger while opening a tin can;

(d) Your favourite pet has been run over;

(e) Your parents have just told you off for staying out late;

(f) Your favourite teacher has criticised you for not working hard enough and you feel that the whole world is against you;

(g) You've just had a letter saying you didn't get the job at last week's interview;

(h) You've been accused of stealing some money in the changing rooms and nobody so far believes you are innocent. The head has sent for you;

(i) You are a blind person about to cross the road;

(j) You are lost in the desert and have no more water.

Further development

1. This is what I call advanced GCSE work. It won't suit every group but it's well worth trying. We're now going to experiment with 'silent' help. Get the group to sit in a circle and put on a tape of Ravel's *Daphnis and Chloe* Suite No. 2 – 'Daybreak'. A volunteer goes into the middle of the circle and sits or moves or stands 'in the spirit of the music'. There is no verbal communication. Anybody from the circle may now go in and offer 'help'. The only channel of communication is the facial expression. There is no stimulus except the music and the pupils' own imagination. Everything is in silent mime . . .

2. Once the pupils have begun to get used to this type of work and are getting into the rhythm of the music, the teacher can say a one-word stimulus. For example, 'fear'. The pupil in the middle then has to obey and reveal that feeling in his or her movements. Help must be forthcoming from the rest of the group. But no more than four people at any one time. No words. Movement, mime, gesture and facial expression.

3. Other suggested one-word stimuli are:

frustration;   startled;
rage;   burning;
lost;   blind.
cold;

Other suitable pieces of music for this kind of work are: Holst –*The Planet Suite*, 'Mars'; Prokofiev – *Classical Symphony No. 1*, second movement; Shostakovitch – *Symphony No. 1*, third movement.

24 Loop dialogues

• Age range: 13–16 • Key words: memory training, concentration, performance skills

I'm going to give each group a loop dialogue to commit to memory and perform. A loop dialogue is a short piece of conversation which you have to learn by heart and repeat as soon as you get to the end.

You keep repeating the dialogue until I stop you, without laughing and in exactly the same way every time with no variation whatsoever. You also repeat any movement, gesture or facial expression in exactly the same order each time.

I'm going to give each group five minutes to learn their dialogue then you must put down the script and perform.

TEACHER'S NOTES

1. Photocopy the desired extracts and give one out to each group. Go round helping the groups with setting.

2. After the first round of performances, suggest that the same dialogue must now be repeated in slow motion.

3. After they have mastered the repetition in slow motion, suggest they now rehearse the same scene in fast motion, like a speeded-up film.

4. When they've mastered this particular exercise suggest they repeat the scene without the sound, as if someone has turned the volume down.

5. At any time during the performance the teacher can call out 'freeze', which pupils must obey on command. Like a freeze frame on a video.

6. When they have mastered the dialogue completely the teacher can then experiment with fast rewind. They have to go backwards like a video film which is rewound to the beginning. It's more difficult than it sounds. The film loop can restart in normal mode as soon as they reach the beginning.

7. The educational value of this exercise is to stress the importance of being totally absorbed by one's character and having the technical ability to repeat a given performance. This is not only useful for memory-training but also for the school play and GCSE prepared performances.

Loop dialogues

(for groups of 2)

1. Sherlock Holmes
2. Classroom Scene
3. The Hairdresser's

(for groups of 3)

4. The Restaurant
5. Agatha Christie
6. Melodrama
7. Pub
8. Museum

Further development

When each group has perfected its particular loop dialogue to the teacher's satisfaction, try the following:

1. Get the pupils to start their dialogues again but this time, instead of repeating, ask them to continue the dialogue and develop it into a story. They should treat it as a piece of prepared improvisation.

2. Ask the pupils to think about what happened before the loop dialogue started and the events leading up to it. They should discuss in their groups how the situation in the loop dialogue could have arisen, then play a scene or scenes which lead into the loop dialogue and end there. They should remember the loop dialogue is fixed and blocked already and must be kept that way.

3. After they've done this, the teacher could ask pupils to prepare a complete scenario of what happened before, then move on to the loop dialogue, and then the conclusion . . .

1. SHERLOCK HOLMES

Holmes: (*seeing something on the floor and bending down to pick it up*) Aha! What's this?

Watson: (*pointing*) It's a hat pin, Holmes.

Holmes: More than just a hat pin, Watson.

Watson: (*looking closer*) My God, Holmes!

Holmes: (*triumphantly*) Exactly, Watson.

Watson: (*dumbfounded*) It's got blood on it!

Holmes: (*head turning sharply to door, in a hoarse whisper, finger to lips*) Quiet!

Watson: What is it?

(*They both listen.*)

(*End of loop dialogue. Start again.*)

2. CLASSROOM SCENE

Teacher: (*pointing at pupil*) Stand up ⎯⎯⎯ .

Pupil: (*standing up trembling*) Yes, sir/miss?

Teacher: (*holding up an exercise book*) Is this supposed to be your homework?

Pupil: My dog chewed it up, sir/miss.

Teacher: (*slamming the exercise book on the desk*) Well, you can jolly well buy another one!

Pupil: Can't afford it, sir/miss.

Teacher: Sit down!

(*Pupil sits.*)

(*End of loop dialogue. Start again.*)

3. THE HAIRDRESSER'S

(*Hairdresser is standing up, cutting customer's hair, customer is sitting.*)

Customer: (*standing up suddenly*) Ow! You've snipped my ear!

Hairdresser: (*apologetically*) I'm so sorry madam/sir.

Customer: (*looking in the mirror*) Look, it's bleeding.

Hairdresser: A thousand apologies, madam/sir.

Customer: I want to see the manager.

Hairdresser: I am the manager.

Customer: Well, you should be fired.

Hairdresser: Please sit down, madam/sir, I'll try again.

(*Customer sits down.*)

(*End of loop dialogue. Start again.*)

4. THE RESTAURANT

Waiter/Waitress: Table for two?

Customer 1: Yes.

Waiter/Waitress: This way please.

(*Waiter/Waitress takes them to a table.*)

Here we are.

(*They sit.*)

Would you like to see a menu?

Customer 2: Yes, please.

(*Waiter/Waitress takes a step away when Customer 1 snaps.*)

Customer 1: This tablecloth's dirty!

Customer 2: Don't make a fuss.

Customer 1: Have you got another table?

Waiter/Waitress: I'm afraid not.

Customer 1: Then we're leaving.

(*Customer 1 stomps out, followed lamely by Customer 2.*)

Customer 2: (*to waiter/waitress on the way out*) So sorry about this.

Waiter/Waitress (*to Customer 2*) It's you I'm sorry for.

(*End of loop dialogue. Start again.*)

5. AGATHA CHRISTIE

(*The scene should be played in the style of Agatha Christie.*)

Detective: (*to Suspect 1*) And where were you on the evening of the 15th?

Suspect 1: I was here, Inspector, in this very room.

Detective: (*pointing at Suspect 1*) You're lying. There was nobody in this room on the 15th.

Suspect 2: How do you know that?

Detective: Because everybody was on holiday.

Suspect 2: You're right, Inspector. (*pointing at Suspect 1*) He/she did it. He/she committed the murder.

Suspect 1: You little pig! (*pointing*) It was you!

(*End of loop dialogue. Start again.*)

6. MELODRAMA

(*In the style of exaggerated Victorian melodrama.*)

Villain: (*hands going for heroine's throat*) I have you now, my sweetling.

Heroine: No! Unhand me!.

Hero: (*entering with gun*) Unhand her, villain!

Villain: And who might you be?

Hero: (*hand on heart*) I am to be . . . her husband.

Heroine: (*hand on heart*) Oh, Godfrey!

Hero: (*hand on heart*) Oh, Rose Marie!

Heroine: (*hand on heart*) Oh, Godfrey!

Hero: (*hand on heart*) Oh, Rose Marie!

Villain: Oh, bugger!

(*End of loop dialogue. Start again.*)

7. PUB

Drunk: (*finishing off pint of beer and slamming glass on counter*) Another pint of bitter, please, landlord.

Barman: (*leaning across counter*) Don't you think you've had enough?

City gent: (*confidently*) A whisky and soda, please, landlord.

Drunk: (*to City gent*) Go away, snob. I'm being served.

Barman: (*to City gent*) Can you wait just a second, please?

City gent: Really! This place is going to the dogs.

(*End of loop dialogue. Start again.*)

8. MUSEUM

Child: (*pointing to valuable object*) Ooh, look!

Parent: Don't point, dear. It's rude.

Attendant: Don't touch the exhibits, please.

Child: How much is it worth then?

Attendant: (*under his breath*) More than you are.

Parent: What did you say?

Attendant: Nothing.

Parent: Must you be so rude?

Child: Shall I hit him/her for you mummy/daddy?

Attendant: Kindly control your child, madam (sir).

(*End of loop dialogue. Start again.*)

Text stimuli for GCSE work

25   Trixie and Baba

Baba: Oh Trix . . . Trix . . . this is . . . must be . . . make or break year . . .

Trixie: You can do it. I've always said you can.

Baba: But what? What?

Trixie: Doesn't matter.

Baba: 'Course it matters.

Trixie: It doesn't as long as you do it . . .

Baba: It matters . . .

Trixie: I'll stand by you.

Baba: But I don't know what to do.

Trixie: Your novel.

Baba: I've got two in my head. Which one shall I write first?

Trixie: The second, the second . . .

Baba: But that would make it the first.

Trixie: Never mind. Get on with it.

Baba: I can't abandon the business. A novel is a full-time job.

Trixie: To hell with the business. It's you that's important. Sell up. We'll go somewhere.

Baba: No. I've got the ruddy boy now. We can't just send him away.

Trixie: Yes, we can.

Baba: No, I'm geared for the export order.

Trixie: It will never come. It might not . . . Oh, you make me sick. (*She pours him tea.*)

Baba: Alright, I'm weak. Weak. But someone's got to take the responsibility. The poor old bugger upstairs, the baby.

Trixie: We'll manage, get on . . .

Baba: You live in a dream world.

Trixie: You live in a dream world, and I always get the blame.

Baba: I s'pose so. Ta. (*Drinks tea*) Yeah . . . yeah . . . God . . . God knows . . .(*Silence*) Do you remember Honiton Nellie?

Trixie: Yes.

Baba: Perhaps I should have gone away with her.

Trixie: I wish you had. Get it out of your system.

Baba: You don't. You tried to stop me.

Trixie: No.

Baba: Yes.

Trixie: I threw you out.

Baba: Yes – it's a threat . . .

Trixie: I said . . .

Baba: You said don't come back . . .

Trixie: Well, what do you expect? You can't have it every way.

Baba: Why not? Why not? Some men do . . .

Trixie: Men. Are you man enough? Why do you listen to me?

Baba: I don't. I keep telling you to shut up.

Trixie: I know.

Baba: That's the first step. If I can shut you up. Perhaps I can think clearly.

Trixie: By all means . . .

Baba: What?

Trixie: By all means, I said.

Baba: Shut up.

Trixie: Certainly. (*She pours him more tea. He scratches.*)

Baba: Old Nell . . . Young Nell . . . young Nell . . . she might have . . . filled the springs of my . . . I might have done that novel with her.

Trixie: Well, bloody well do it – with anybody – don't get on at me all the time that's all. You make me nervous.

Baba: I know. It's the artistic temperament.

Trixie: I've got one as well.

Baba: Ohh God . . .

Trixie: I have . . .

Baba: Alright . . .

Trixie: I have started writing my life story . . .

Baba: Mmmmmm . . .

Trixie: The trials and tribulations of married life.

From *Trixie and Baba* by John Antrobus (John Calder).

TEACHER'S NOTES

1. Photocopy the extract for as many pupils as you have.

2. Explain that this passage is about two people who do not get on and ask the pupils to read it through aloud with a partner and discuss the possible reasons for the tension between them.

3. Go round listening and helping with suggestions. Encourage any positive ideas.

4. Ask each pair to develop the story into a short improvisation lasting three to four minutes. It can be a husband and wife talking, or two brothers, or two sisters, or two friends. The important thing is for there to be conflict and reasons for that conflict. Tell them they don't necessarily have to use the names of the characters in the passage; they can do so if they wish or they can use their own real-life names, or make up names.

   They should decide *where* the scene is going to take place. In the kitchen? The lounge? The bedroom? At what time of day or night is it? First thing in the morning? Last thing at night before going to bed? They should think about that, it could be important to the *tone* and *mood* of their improvisation. Explain that people react differently at different times of day.

   It is also important that they think about whether the two characters are on stage together from the beginning of the improvisation – perhaps sitting having breakfast? – or whether one of them is already on stage and the other comes in from outside. If so, they should think about where he/she might come from.

   They should think about the *structure* of their improvisation, especially the beginning and the end. It could end with one character storming out and slamming the door. Point out that a definite ending gives shape and form to a scene.

   Explain that it is important to think about *technical aspects* as well as the content and that good plays and scenes are well structured. They should think in simple terms, and not make it too complicated. Stress that a good play or film has a beginning, a middle and an end. Theirs should not be too long or too short. Three to four minutes is about right.

Ask them to set up their scenes and start rehearsing and discussing. Give them ten minutes.

5. Go round and observe the work. Look for groups who have no starting point and make positive suggestions. They may have problems with the characters. Emphasize the importance of making a decision about husband/wife or brother/sister, otherwise the creative process cannot get off the ground.

If what pupils have chosen is not working suggest they try a different type of relationship. Once the relationship and the location have been fixed, the dialogue ideas should begin to flow.

6. Emphasize the importance of listening to each other in improvisations. Get them to look at the text again if they're stuck and find a line which will give them an idea. For example, 'You live in a dream world' or 'Someone's got to take the responsibility' or 'I can't abandon the business'. Ask them what business these people run. A shop? A restaurant? An art gallery? A fish and chip shop?

7. Stress the structural importance of a definite ending. For example, a character walking out and slamming the door saying, 'I've got to go to work now. I can't stand here arguing with you all day!'; or a response to an offstage sound such as 'Listen, now you've made the baby cry' or 'That's the front door bell. It's probably the milkman wanting his money' or 'It's time I opened the shop'.

8. Stop the rehearsals with enough time for each group to show their improvisations to the rest of the class.

Further development

1. Get pupils to work in groups of five. Emphasize the same structural and character points as above only this time there will be three extra characters who can extend the improvisation into a longer scene or a series of related scenes. The extra characters could be the ones referred to in the text:
   (a) 'I've got the ruddy boy now.' (This could be a son or a shop assistant.);
   (b) 'The poor old bugger upstairs.' (This could be a mother or father. Whose? Possibly sick?);
   (c) 'Do you remember Honiton Nellie?' (She is obviously someone important from the past. She could turn up in the present.);

2. The relationships will now be more complicated so much more discussion on time is necessary within each group. Again, go round and make positive suggestions. If something is not working in dramatic terms tell them, explain why and suggest an alternative. If they don't like your ideas, don't insist. They will find out in performance for themselves what works and what is boring. Just keep stressing the value of a definite structure. Pupils' ideas may be better than yours but their knowledge of structure is likely to be minimal.

3. If a group has too many ideas for one scene suggest they spread them out over two or three scenes, e.g. Scene 1, 9.00am Thursday, Scene, 2 6.30pm Thursday, Scene 3, 3.00pm Saturday; or suggest *one week later* – one of the group could announce the changes.

4. If any of the groups come up with a 'flashback' idea, this should be encouraged as it gives a different viewpoint of the characters. Travelling backwards and forwards in time is one of the most imaginative and interesting aspects of theatre (and film). But again, stress the importance of *simplicity*: Scene 1 in the present, Scene 2 in the past, Scene 3 in the present.

5. Structure their ideas. You could suggest the idea of the husband (Baba) being a writer of romantic fiction. Instead of running his business he locks himself in his room to write. Suggest the idea of enacting a fantasy sequence from one of his 'novels' involving his ex-girlfriend, Honiton Nellie. Music could be used as a transition link with him then being abruptly brought back to reality by his wife calling (see suggested scenario).

6. As pupils get more used to this kind of work they will need less and less 'feeding', but in the initial stages the teacher must provide some ideas if they are lacking in the pupils, especially as regards structure and technique. Here is a suggested scenario which I used with one of my classes based on this particular text. You need not use it in detail (or at all) but some of the ideas might be helpful.

Suggested scenario

Trixie and Baba are married and run a rather tatty antique shop – more of a junk shop. Baba considers himself to be a novelist and lives in a dream world. Instead of managing the business he leaves it to his wife. He fantasizes about his ex-girlfriend, Honiton Nellie, and keeps dreaming about what life could have been like if he'd married her and been a successful writer.

Trixie is rather ordinary and sensible. Her mother's money was used to set up the business. Trixie and Baba are constantly bickering. They have a young assistant who helps in the shop. Baba can't stand him and, in his imagination, sees this chap as a villain and himself as a hero.

A scene from one of Baba's novels could be enacted – possibly a 17th-century musketeer setting or a Zorro-style fencing scene or a Victorian melodrama idea. Baba rescues Honiton from the wicked villain. You could use Tchaikovsky's *Romeo and Juliet* suite (fencing section) for the fight scene and Mozart's *Piano Concerto No. 21* (slow movement) could serve as a background for a slow-motion sequence of Baba running towards Honiton Nellie for the romantic embrace. These scenes are constantly interrupted by Trixie yelling for him to come and do various things.

Stress throughout the importance of making the characters as believable as possible. 'If you believe in the characters so will the audience.'

26 Our day out

(Below the cliff top, the sea is breaking on rocks in a cave mouth. In the distance Mrs Kay is shouting 'Carol, Carol', and Colin is searching the far end of the beach. Carol is standing on top of the cliff watching the waves below. She looks out over the sea. Alone on the cliff top, she is at peace with the warm sun and light breeze upon her – a fleeting moment of tranquillity.)

Briggs: Carol Chandler! *(Briggs approaches. On seeing her he stops and stands a few yards off.)* Just come here.

(She turns and stares at him.)

Who gave you permission to come up here?

Carol: No-one. *(Turning she dismisses him.)*

Briggs: I'm talking to you, Carol Chandler.

(She continues to ignore his presence.)

Now just listen here, young lady . . . *(As he goes to move towards her, she turns on him.)*

Carol: Don't you come near me!

Briggs: *(taken aback, stopping)* Pardon!

Carol: I don't want you to come near me.

Briggs: Well, in that case just get yourself moving and let's get down to the beach.

(Pause)

Carol: You go. I'm not coming.

Briggs: You what?

Carol: Tell Mrs Kay that she can go home without me. I'm stoppin' here . . . In Wales.

(Pause)

Briggs: Now just you listen to me – I've had just about enough today, just about enough, and I'm not putting up with a pile of silliness from the likes of you. Now come on . . .

(*He starts to move towards her. She takes a step towards the edge of the cliff.*)

Carol: Try an' get me an' I'll jump over.

(*Briggs stops, astounded. There is an angry pause. She continues to ignore him.*)

Briggs: Now come on! I'll not tell you again. (*He moves forward. Again, she moves nearer to the edge. He stops and they look at each other.*) I'll give you five seconds. Just five seconds. One . . . two . . . three . . . four . . . I'm warning you . . . five!

(*She stares at him blankly. Briggs stares back in impotent rage.*)

Carol: I've told y' . . . I'm not comin' down with y'.

(*Pause*)

I'll jump y' know . . . I will.

Briggs: Just what are you trying to do to me?

Carol: I've told you. Leave me alone and I won't jump.

(*Pause*)

I wanna stay here. Where it's nice.

Briggs: Stay here? How could you stay here? What would you do? Where would you live?

Carol: I'll be alright.

Briggs: Now I've told you. Stop being so silly.

Carol: (*turning on him*) What do you worry for, eh? Eh? You don't care, do y'? Do y'?

Briggs: What? About you? Listen . . . if I didn't care, why am I here, now, trying to stop you doing something stupid?

Carol: Because if I jumped over, you'll get into trouble when you get back to school. That's why, Briggsy! So stop goin' on. You hate me.

Briggs: Don't be ridiculous – just because I'm a schoolteacher it doesn't mean to say that . . .

Carol: Don't lie, you! I know you hate me. I've seen you goin' home in your car, passin' us on the street. And the way y' look at us. You hate all the kids. (*She turns again to the sea, dismissing him.*)

Briggs: What . . . makes you think that? Eh?

Carol: Why can't I just stay out here, eh? Why can't I live in one of them nice white houses an' do the garden an' that?

Briggs: Look, Carol . . . you're talking as though you've given up on life already. You sound as though life for you is just ending, instead of beginning. Now why can't, I mean, if it's what you want, what's to stop you working hard at school from now on, getting a good job and then moving out here when you're old enough? Eh?

Carol: (*Turns slowly to look at him. Contempt.*) Don't be friggin' stupid. (*She turns and looks down at the sea below.*) It's been a great day today. I loved it. I don't wanna leave here an' go home. (*She moves to the edge of the cliff. Briggs is alarmed but unable to move.*) If I stayed though, it wouldn't be no good. You'd send the coppers to get me.

Briggs: We'd have to. How would you survive out here?

Carol: I know.

(*Pause*)

I'm not goin' back though.

Briggs: Please . . .

Carol: Sir, sir, y' know if you'd been my old feller, I woulda been alright, wouldn't I?

(*Briggs slowly holds out his hand. She moves to the very edge of the cliff. Briggs is aware of how close she is.*)

Briggs: Carol. Carol, please come away from there. (*stretching out his hand to her*) Please.

(*Carol looks at him and a smile breaks across her face.*)

Carol: Sir . . . sir you don't half look funny, y' know.

Briggs: (*smiling back at her*) Why?

Carol: Sir, you should smile more often, y' look great when y' smile.

Briggs: Come on, Carol. (*He gingerly approaches her.*)

Carol: What'll happen to me for doin' this, sir?

Briggs: Nothing. I promise you.

Carol: Sir, y' promisin' now, but what about when we get back t' school?

Briggs: (*almost next to her now*) It won't even be mentioned.

(*She turns and looks down at the drop then back at Briggs's outstretched arm. Carol lifts her hand to his. She slips. Briggs grabs out quickly and manages to pull her up to him. Briggs wraps his arms around her.*)

From *Our Day Out and Other Plays* by Willy Russell (Hutchinson)

TEACHER'S NOTES

1. Ask the class to get into groups of four or five. Give out photocopies of the extract from *Our Day Out* and ask the groups to read it out loud. Any two people in the group can choose to read. It doesn't have to be a boy reading Briggs or a girl reading Carol.

2. After they've finished reading it discuss with the class the theme of the piece – suicide. Ask them to suggest reasons why people can be driven to despair. Write on a blackboard or note all the suggestions on a piece of paper. Try to arrive (with the class) at a succinct definition of suicide.

3. Ask the class to select any of the suggestions put forward and to dramatise in their groups the final moments in the drama of a suicide attempt. What we are aiming for is to go straight to the end of the story where we see the suicide attempt as a 'frozen tableau' and then we go back to the beginning and follow a normal chronological sequence of events, explaining the final outcome.

   This is a dramatic and arresting method in which to start a play or improvisation where we are plunged immediately into the action. Shakespeare uses this technique in some of his plays, for example in *Macbeth* where we are thrown right into the midst of the action with the three witches. This technique is sometimes called 'in media res', Latin for 'in the middle of things'.

   So get the groups to decide on the way in which the suicide makes the attempt – jumping off a roof, hanging, taking pills, shooting, etc. They will come up with lots of 'cheerful' suggestions. Get them to 'freeze frame' the final moments.

4. Having decided the ending, a group discussion follows on the relationships between the characters and the way in which each character has affected the other. You could read J.B. Priestley's *An Inspector Calls* where each character has contributed somehow to the eventual suicide of Eva Smith.

5. Point out to the class the final stage directions in the *Our Day Out* extract: 'She turns and looks down at the drop then back at Briggs's outstretched arm. Carol lifts her hand to his. She slips. Briggs grabs out quickly and manages to pull her to him. Briggs wraps his arms round her.' This dramatic moment could be enacted at the beginning of a play which then leads up to it. So try to get them to think in these terms. A dramatic

100

opening, a return to explain, and the same scene as an ending. In this way their work will have a structure and a solid framework.

6. A workshop idea for *Our Day Out*:

(a) Discuss with the whole class where they might like to go out if they had the opportunity. Somewhere in their part of the country. It doesn't have to be the same as in the play (i.e. Conway Castle). Write on the blackboard or note down all the suggestions given;

(b) Ask the class to get into groups of three. One of them is teacher and the other two are pupils. They have to improvise a scene in which the pupils return to the teacher (who had sent them to get a concensus of opinion from their class about where the class might like to go out) and let him/her know the outcome. Starting line: 'The class say they'd like to go out to ---- Sir';

(c) The teachers from each group now play a scene together (in the staff room at break or lunchtime) where they all discuss the pupils' suggestions for the various 'days out'. A sum of money has been donated by the County Council for educational school trips;

(d) The pupils from each group now do a scene together in which they talk about what's been decided so far. They also talk about the personalities of their teachers and their attitudes;

(e) The teacher who has chosen the most boring venue for the day out (in my workshop it was a library) and appears to be the most conservative, unimaginative and intolerant person now performs a scene with any two pupils in which they tell him/her that they do not wish to go to the library but to a fairground;

(f) Two other pupils (smokers) perform a scene in which they go through every single suggestion made so far and say it's boring, but they don't say where they want to go;

(g) Two other pupils are sent for by the Briggs-type teacher who tells them that the trip to the library will be far cheaper than all the other places they want to go to;

(h) All the teachers are discussing the situation so far and a verbal slanging match ensues between 'Briggs' and a set of more liberal teachers;

(i) A scene between the pupils in which they talk about the shouting that took place in the staff room and a fight that occurred between 'Briggs' and another, very liberal, teacher who believes in 'treating the kids like adults';

(j) Assembly. All the teachers and all the pupils are in this scene. The headteacher (a weak person) takes the assembly and hands over to

'Briggs' who announces that the 'Days Out' have been cancelled due to bad behaviour in the school. Boos and catcalls. Detentions are given out;

(k) The pupils are sitting around dejected in their classroom. The liberal teacher comes in and tells them he/she has persuaded the Head that the Day Out can go ahead after all. Cheers and jubilation.

Working in this way with the whole class involved – either acting or watching – brings out characteristics in the pupils which reveal to the teacher the particular part each will be suitable for if a production of *Our Day Out* is envisaged.

Further development

1. This scene is about relationships: the way we relate to other people. The dramatic nature of the situation, the urgency of trying to save somebody's life forces Mr Briggs to come out of his shell and for one brief moment to smile naturally. His outstretched hand is a symbol as well as a fact of selfless action. He wants to save Carol from jumping to death. He is being a real human being at last, not a teacher-machine. Even though, as Carol has guessed, he'd get into trouble if one of his pupils committed suicide, he is still more concerned for her safety than his own. It is the first step in the humanisation of Briggs. Later in the play he relaxes completely and is natural with the kids. But it's only a temporary phase. He cannot bear to expose himself to the light of day so he therefore ruins the film of himself enjoying himself. He goes back to being the teacher-machine.

2. Explain that it sometimes takes a dramatic incident or an unusual situation before people will start to communicate. Ask pupils to work on some improvisation ideas where it's important to 'let go':

(a) Pupils should get into pairs. One is a very 'enclosed' teacher like Mr Briggs and the other is a pupil waiting outside the office. The pupil is not wearing his/her tie or some other item of school uniform. The teacher starts to lay into him/her, threatening punishments, giving dire warnings, quoting the school rules, etc. What the teacher doesn't know is that the pupil's mother has just died of cancer. Pupils should develop the scene through improvisation;

(b) Again in pairs, the same characters. This time the pupil is hauled out to the front in assembly and exposed to the whole school as a person who is utterly disobedient because he/she has a slovenly appearance. What the teacher doesn't know is that the pupil's father has just lost his job and there is no money coming in to buy anything;

(c) The same characters are on a school trip and the pupil cannot be found. Eventually the pupil is traced to a window ledge where he/she is threatening to jump. The teacher has to try to persuade the pupil to come in.

The above could also be tackled in groups of four as a sequence involving four characters: a pupil, a liberal teacher, a Briggs type and a headteacher.

27 Macbeth

(Enter three Murderers.)

First Murderer: But who did bid thee join with us?
Third Murderer: Macbeth.
Second Murderer: He needs not our mistrust, since he delivers
   Our offices and what we have to do
   To the direction just.
First Murderer: Then stand with us;
   The west yet glimmers with some streaks of day.
   Now spurs the lated traveller apace
   To gain the timely inn; and near approaches
   The subject of our watch.
Third Murderer: Hark, I hear horses!
Banquo: *(within)* Give us a light there, ho!
Second Murderer: Then 'tis he. The rest
   That are within the note of expectation
   Already are i' the court.
First Murderer: His horses go about.
Third Murderer: Almost a mile; but he does usually.
   So all men do, from hence to the palace gate
   Made it their walk.

(Enter Banquo and Fleance with a torch.)

Second Murderer: A light, a light!
Third Murderer: 'Tis he.
First Murderer: Stand to't!
Banquo: It will be rain tonight!
First Murderer: Let it come down!

(They attack Banquo.)

Banquo: O treachery! Fly, good Fleance, fly, fly, fly!
   Thou mayst revenge – O slave!

(Banquo falls. Fleance escapes.)

Third Murderer: Who did strike out the light?
First Murderer: Was't not the way?

Third Murderer: There's but one down; the son is fled.
Second Murderer: We have lost best half of our affair.
First Murderer: Well, let's away and say how much is done.

(*Exeunt.*)

Act 3 Scene 3 of *Macbeth* by William Shakespeare (Penguin)

TEACHER'S NOTES

1. Ask the class to get into groups of five. Each member of the group has to play a role in the scene – either Murderer 1, 2 or 3, Banquo or Fleance. Give out photocopies of the extract to each group and tell them the task is to re-write the scene completely in modern English and to change the time and place to an inner city of the 1990s. The horses can become cars (or motorbikes), the fire torches can become electric torches, etc. Instead of 'murderers', suggest they are 'muggers'. Each person has to learn his/her lines by heart and then act out the scene. Remember the costumes will be modern too.

2. Action sequences require much thought and pre-planning in the theatre. 'Killing' somebody effectively on stage is not as simple as it may appear and it would be as well to discuss with pupils the careful and meticulous planning that a 'fight director' has to engage in before a simple murder on stage 'looks realistic'.

   One is hampered here by the over-exposure to television of many pupils, for whom violence and death are linked to 'stunt' work, and specifically filmic technique as opposed to stage technique.

   Effective technique for action sequences in the theatre (and the drama studio) does not necessarily have to follow the rhythm of life. If Banquo is just knocked down and jumped upon by a group of thugs who then proceed to put the boot in – it will appear messy on stage. Strangely enough it won't seem 'realistic' even though the pupils probably feel it to be realistic. So the first rule for action or fight scenes in the theatre has got to be 'Don't follow your natural impulses'.

   A simple stage direction like 'They attack Banquo' must be thought out. How do they attack Banquo? All together? One at a time? Who actually stabs him? All of them at the same time? All of them at different times? Is Banquo held down while another stabs him? Do they circle around him first or do they attack straight away? What would be the most effective on stage? Would a pause serve any purpose? Does Banquo see the faces of any of the murderers before he dies? As he is dying?

3. Ask the groups to 'choreograph' the murder of Banquo according to a strict plan – decide who is going to stab, when and how. Then suggest to the pupils that they experiment with stylized movement:

(a) commit the murder in fluid slow motion;
(c) commit the murder in normal motion;
(c) commit the murder in fast motion.

What is the difference between these three techniques? Which one appears 'right'?

4. Changes in rhythm and pace always provide interest in the theatre, not only in the way the dialogue is spoken but in the way action sequences are devised. Ask the pupils to think in terms of Banquo and Fleance acting like 'hunted stags brought to bay' – realizing they are surrounded they quickly try to escape, then another murderer comes out and they slowly walk backwards; they try to escape via another route, another murderer emerges, etc. This quick movement, slow movement has strong dramatic impact on stage if it is rehearsed carefully and can lead to a stunning climax (the murder) with a short pause before the knives come down (or the guns fire).

Further development

Here are some improvisation ideas for bringing the situation of the play *Macbeth* into the twentieth century and making it more relevant and meaningful to modern pupils.

1. Macbeth is a business man working for a big computer firm. He is young, ambitious and has accomplished many profitable deals for the company and lined his own pockets with all the accoutrements of gracious 20th-century living – a BMW, smart mews house in central London (as well as a country estate in Wiltshire), all the latest electronic equipment, expensive clothes, etc. His wife is also young and ambitious and wants her husband to be top man at the computer firm, to replace the old 'fuddy duddy' managing director who is very old-fashioned and boring. Unfortunately, the managing director has two sons whom he wants to take over from him when he retires. Mrs Macbeth dabbles in the occult and knows various psychics and mediums who have prophesied that her

husband will one day be managing director. She takes her husband to see one of them.

(a) Get the pupils to improvise a scene around the visit of Mr and Mrs Macbeth to the medium. Is Macbeth cynical or is he a believer in the occult?

(b) Pupils should then improvise a scene between Mr and Mrs Macbeth after the visit to the medium in which Mrs Macbeth urges her husband to kill the managing director and take over the whole firm.

(c) Finally they can improvise a scene in which Mr and Mrs Macbeth invite the managing director to dinner and dispose of him by the end of the evening. How do they kill him?

Groups of four for the whole sequence: Mr and Mrs Macbeth, Medium, the Boss.

2. Another modern approach would be to make Macbeth belong to a Mafia gang. Through his ruthlessness and clear thinking he achieves high status within the crime syndicate. One day he is passing a gypsy flower seller in the street who tells him he will be 'il capo' one day soon. When Macbeth relays this to his wife they start to plot the overthrow of the leader 'Duncano'.

28 Waiting gentlewoman

(*The un-named waiting gentlewoman in* Macbeth *is speaking ...*)

If Daddy had known the set up,
I'm absolutely positive, he'd never
Have let me come. Honestly,
The whole thing's too gruesome
For words. There's nobody here to talk to
At all. Well, nobody under about ninety,
I mean. All the possible men have buggered
Off to the other side, and the rest,
Poor old dears, they'd have buggered off
Too, if their poor old legs would have
Carried them. HM's a super person, of course,
But she's a bit seedy just now,
Quite different from how marvellous she was
At the Coronation. And this doctor they've got in –
Well, he's only an ordinary little GP,
With a very odd accent, and even I
Can see that what HM needs is
A real psychiatrist. I mean, all this about
Blood and washing. Definitely Freudian.
As for Himself, well, definitely
Not my type. Daddy's got this thing
About self-made men, of course, that's why
He was keen for me to come. But I think
He's gruesome. What HM sees in him
I cannot imagine. And he talks to himself.
That's so rude, I always think.
I hope Daddy comes for me soon.

From *Selected Poems* by U.A. Fanthorpe (Peterloo Poets)

TEACHER'S NOTES

1. Ask the class to get into groups of three and to read Act 5 Scene 1 of
   Macbeth – the sleepwalking scene. Each person in the group takes on a

particular role, either Doctor, Gentlewoman or Lady Macbeth. It matters not a jot if it's three boys, three girls or a mixed group.

2. Ask the groups to work on the following improvisation after they have read the scene through:
A hospital ward. A nurse is on night duty. She walks round the ward with a torch checking that all the patients are asleep. Senior doctor comes in and asks if everything is alright. The nurse says yes and the doctor decides to go home. As soon as the doctor leaves, one of the patients begins to stir and quietly rises from the bed and, with eyes open and staring, goes over to a sink and starts to wash his hands. The nurse tells him to get back to bed but the patient is oblivious to anything. The nurse realizes that the patient is in some kind of trance and that it might be dangerous to wake him up, so she lets him alone. The patient eventually goes back to bed. Next day the nurse tells the doctor what happened. The doctor is sceptical but agrees to stay up that night and watch with the nurse. Nothing happens that night and the doctor is very annoyed at having lost so much sleep. She tells the nurse that it must have been her imagination.

Next day the doctor checks the patient's temperature, blood pressure, etc. and can find nothing wrong with him. What is the patient in hospital for? Each group has to decide this for themselves. It could be for a gall stone operation or the removal of an appendix – anything the group thinks appropriate.

That night the nurse is on duty again and the same thing happens. The patient gets up, walks to the sink and starts to wash his hands but this time he is talking to himself, mumbling something about 'I shouldn't have killed him, I shouldn't have done it . . .'.

Again the nurse tells the doctor and the doctor, much against her natural inclination, agrees to sit up again. Nothing happens. The doctor is furious and threatens to sack the nurse.

The next night the patient walks again when the nurse is on her own, this time speaking even louder and appearing very agitated. The next night the nurse begs the doctor to sit up with her again and after much protest she agrees to do it, but for the last time. If nothing happens, the nurse will lose her job.

3. In groups of four, pupils should look at the poem 'Waiting Gentlewoman'. Ask them the following questions:

- What class of person is the gentlewoman in this poem?
- Is it a modern setting? How do they know?

- What job do they think 'Macbeth' does?
- Where do the characters live?
- What is the job of the gentlewoman?
- What kind of person is the doctor?
- What has gone wrong with HM's marriage?
- How old is 'Himself'?
- Which words show the gentlewoman as belonging to a particular class?
- What kind of 'accent' does the doctor have?
- If 'Himself' is a self-made man, what has he made his money from?
- How long is the gentlewoman going to spend here? Is she under contract? Why has her father sent her here?
- What does 'Freudian' mean in this context?

Pupils should then use the poem as the basis for an improvisation following the pattern of scenes as follows:

Scene 1: 'Daddy' sees advert in the paper for job as . . . and suggests his daughter applies for it because of the social kudos it might bring.

Scene 2: Gentlewoman interviewed by 'Himself'. She gets the job.

Scene 3: Gentlewoman meets her 'patient' for the first time. She appears normal.

Scene 4: Gentlewoman awoken by noise at night and sees 'strange happenings'.

Scene 5: Gentlewoman tells doctor about what she saw but doctor doesn't believe her.

Scene 6: Gentlewoman phones 'Daddy' to ask if she can come back home. He says no, she must stick with it.

Scene 7: Dinner scene. Present are: Himself, HM, Doctor and Gentlewoman.

Scene 8: Gentlewoman sees and hears HM sleepwalking and muttering 'Out damned spot'.

Scene 9: Gentlewoman phones up Daddy and tells him she thinks HM has murdered someone and has a guilty conscience. Daddy tells her not to be so stupid.

Scene 10: Gentlewoman persuades doctor to wait up with her to see HM sleepwalking.

Each group should supply their own ending.

4. Ask each group of three to put Act 5 Scene 1 into modern colloquial English. Each person can write down his/her own words and the group rehearses the scene as for a performance. At the end of the scene ask the

groups to continue with another episode which does not occur in the actual play:

The Gentlewoman follows Lady Macbeth out and back to her room. She starts to remove all objects from the room which might serve as potential suicide aids i.e. daggers, sharp implements, plus anything else she can think of. Next morning, the Gentlewoman asks Lady Macbeth if she remembers anything about last night. Starting line: 'Did you sleep well last night, Ma'am?'

5. Using the poem 'Waiting Gentlewoman' as a basis for a master-servant or patient-nurse relationship, pupils should work on the following improvisation ideas in groups of three:
   (a) 'I'm looking after my eccentric aunt who is wealthy and might leave me a lot of money but, my God, she's difficult';
   (b) 'I'm looking after my boss's wife who is bedridden except when she sleep walks and starts jabbering about her husband having murdered somebody;
   (c) 'I hate working in this lunatic asylum where even the doctors are a bit strange and the patients seem to harbour guilty secrets when they talk and sometimes walk in their sleep.'

29 Valuable

(After reading two paragraphs in a newspaper)

All these illegitimate babies . . .
Oh, girls, girls,
Silly little cheap things,
Why do you not put some value on yourselves,
Learn to say, No?
Did nobody teach you?
Nobody teaches anybody to say No nowadays,
People should teach people to say No.

Oh, poor panther,
Oh, you poor black animal,
At large for a few moments in a school
For young children in Paris,
Now in your cage again,
How your great eyes bulge with bewilderment,
There is something there that accuses us,
In your angry and innocent eyes,
Something that says:
I am too valuable to be kept in a cage.

Oh, these illegitimate babies!
Oh, girls, girls,
Silly little valuable things,
You should have said, 'No, I am valuable',
And again, 'It is because I am valuable
I say, No'.

Nobody teaches anybody they are valuable nowadays.

Girls, you are valuable,
And you, panther, you are valuable,
But the girls say: 'I shall be alone
If I say "I am valuable" and other people do not say it of me,
I shall be alone, there is no comfort there.'
No, it is not comforting but it is valuable,
And if everybody says it in the end
It will be comforting. And for the panther too,

If everybody says he is valuable
It will be comforting for him.

From *Collected Poems* by Stevie Smith (Penguin)

TEACHER'S NOTES

1. After giving out photocopies of the poem to all members of the class try to lead a discussion on what they regard as valuable. What is important to them? What is of value to one person may not be of value to another.

   Ask each person in the class to make a list of five things he/she regards as valuable, in order of importance, e.g. family, cat, video, television, etc. Each pupil has then to hand in the list to the teacher, without putting a name on it. The teacher picks one out at random and says, 'This person regards . . . as being the most valuable thing in his/her life. Let's have a television forum on this. Who wants to be chairperson?'

2. After a certain amount of arguing and airing opinions, the teacher (or the chairperson) can sum up by pointing out that something is only important if people feel strongly about it. Emotions have to be involved. What gets them mad? What stirs them to indignation, anger, adoration, resentment, fear? That is what is valuable to them. Do they feel strongly about conservation, atomic weapons, Christianity, child abuse, the death penalty, cruelty to animals, mugging old ladies, race prejudice? What is it that really bugs them? Ask the class, one by one, to stand up and say what they really can't bear – whether it's the latest fashion or green wellies, whatever. Tell them they can rant and rave and really let themselves go.

3. This lively approach should bring about a healthy response. If not, try it with each pupil sounding off at the same time, talking to an imaginary person or audience (though this will be loud!). We are preparing the class for more concentrated group exercises and endeavouring to arouse the emotions in a structured way.

4. Now ask the class to get into pairs. They must each find something that makes them really emotional and indignant. They should not be boring and say that there's nothing that gets under their skin. There must be. Even if it's something petty, they should bring it out into the open. Even if it's the way their brother or sister slurps tea or the way their teacher dresses, they must bring it out into the light of day and not keep it hidden.

Tell them to put themselves into a situation where they can really let fling at this person. They should say what they really feel. Their partner is this other person but their partner will be shouting at them too. Neither of them should listen to the other but just think about getting whatever it is off their chest.

Cover your ears and when they're really into it, stop them and say they are now going to have a heated argument with each other. They don't wish to be heard by a third party 'off stage' so they are speaking as quietly but intensely as possible. They are:

(a) Two pupils. One of them has smashed a window but their teacher is going to expel them both if they don't own up. The teacher is standing just outside the door;
(b) Two waiters or waitresses in dispute about who should serve the 'Queen' when she comes to dinner that night. Their boss is just outside the door and has threatened to sack them both if there is any more arguing;
(c) A married couple arguing about a divorce, but they don't wish to be heard by their children who are sleeping next door. One of them is very seriously ill.

They should then make some of their own situations as well.

5. By this time, pupils should be ready to work from the poem 'Valuable'. It is best not to approach this poem 'cold' but to do some lead-up work first, as above. Now they can work in groups of four or five on their own ideas from the poem, or on any of the following:

(a) A fifteen-year-old girl announces to her very strict, middle-class parents that she is pregnant. The father of the child turns out to be someone the parents despise either because he is from a very working-class family or because he is a foreigner or has a different religion. Pupils should devise their own conclusion. What does each person prize as valuable?;
(b) A sixteen-year-old boy discovers that his sister is pregnant by his best friend. He is very attached to his sister especially since their father died but he is also great mates with his best friend. Should he tell their mother? Does the mother know already or not? How should he tackle the best friend? What does he regard as most valuable? Groups should work out the motivations of the different characters and experiment with improvisation to arrive at some value judgements for each character;
(c) A circus owner treats his/her animals with little affection. An escaped

panther is found half-dead, half-starved in a school playground by two pupils. The pupils contact a journalist who is doing a series of articles about cruelty to circus animals. The journalist approaches the circus owner. What does each character regard as valuable? The circus owner: money. The journalist: his/her story. The pupils: the panther. Role play and character should dictate the story and the sequence of scenes.

Further development

1. Use the line 'People should teach people to say No' as a starting point for various value judgement improvisations:

   (a) 'No' to stealing
   In groups of three one pupil is a person who is tempted to steal in a supermarket. The other two in the group represent the devil and the good angel who offer arguments for and against stealing. The outcome depends on how persuasive the two 'airy combatants' can be. Being 'bodiless' they cannot touch the person, of course;

   (b) 'No' to stealing cigarettes
   A young boy or girl is tempted to steal his/her parents' cigarettes. Treat as above;

   (c) 'No' to being part of a gang
   The person here is beginning to be an individual and no longer wishes to lose his/her identity as part of a gang. Pupils should work in groups of four or five. The film *Rebel without a Cause* is an excellent way of demonstrating the theme of 'what is valuable'. The main character says 'no' to what the gang expect. Get pupils to work in the context of a character saying 'no' to a gang:

in a cafe;	in a prison;
on a street corner;	on a beach;
at a disco;	on a housing estate.

2. Pupils should read *The Proposal* by Anton Chekhov. In groups of three they can work on the theme of a character proposing marriage to a young woman because:

   she is rich;
   she is pretty;
   she is from a higher social class;
   he is in love with her.

Similarly they can work from the woman's point of view on the theme of rejecting the marriage proposal because:

he is unattractive;
he is poor;
he is from a lower social class;
or accepting it because she loves him.

The extra character in each case is the father or mother of the girl.

30 Teaching practice

Thwack! Go on, get out of here, and don't come back!
. . . I treat them all like that, that's all they understand –
And they respect you for it, mark my words.
In forty years I've never had a rowdy class – not once!

Forget that nonsense that they teach you in your
Education Course. Those lecturers don't know the score,
The simple fact that most kids just aren't human beings at all,
They're animals. They don't respond to kindness, trust –

A whip and a chair is more their mark. You've got to scare
The little brutes. Yes, scare them rigid, make them live
In fear of you. That's discipline . . .

Hey – You! . . . Did you see that? That little beast was spying,
Listening to every word I've said. Go on – yes, run!
Quick! . . . Bring him back – See me tomorrow morning after play.
That's how it's done! You're learning fast –
You'll be alright.

From *So Far So Good* by Mick Gowar (Collins)

TEACHER'S NOTES

1. Here we have the question of discipline. A school setting is appropriate to the theme but ask for and discuss other areas where discipline is important – the armed forces, sport, the police force, the circus, the training of a doctor or surgeon, music, the art of acting, etc.

2. Ask the class what discipline is. Write up all the various answers on a blackboard if possible or get them to write them down in their drama note books. Say, 'I want to arrive at a definition of the word discipline with you'.

3. Ask for examples where too much discipline can be a bad thing – a parent demanding too much of a child, an army officer spilling over into cruelty, a religion that kills all the fun in life, an earnest teacher with no sense of humour.

4. As a start I'd recommend you give each pupil in the group a character word card and ask them to think of that character in terms of:

(a) discipline;
(b) lack of discipline;
(c) too much discipline.

Mime an action by the character which implies a disciplined approach to life. If the character on the card is not appropriate then call out the following characters and ask the group to enact them in the three different ways indicated above:

(a) a goalkeeper;   (e) a secretary;
(b) a guard;   (f) a diamond cutter;
(c) a hairdresser;   (g) a teacher.
(d) a cameraman;

In each case call out stimuli such as: 'Let me have a disciplined hairdresser please . . . now without any exaggeration an undisciplined hairdresser. Now a hairdresser who has too much discipline. What would she/he do if she/he had too much discipline? Become too demanding of others as well as herself/himself? Irritable? Anti-social? Obnoxious?

Pupils should now get into pairs and, as you call out the stimuli, start to formulate a scene between the character and anyone else they think appropriate. For example, the cameraman could be working with an actor, the teacher working with another colleague or a pupil.

5. In pairs again, ask them to adopt the roles of parent and child. The parent tells off the child with the starting line, 'You've got no discipline, that's your problem'. Then attempt the reverse with the child accusing the parent of lack of discipline.

6. Now start to work towards the characters in the poem: a young teacher and an older, experienced teacher.

(a) Ask each pair to write a monologue to introduce themselves, e.g. 'I am Sandra Baines. I am 21 years old and I've just left the polytechnic with a qualification that allows me to teach Maths and PE. This is my first job', or 'I am Douglas Foster. I am 58 years old. My subject is History. I've been teaching for thirty years, twenty of them in tough inner city schools where the children are like animals. They can't help acting like animals because their parents have brought them up that way, but this is a game of survival and I'm making damned sure that it's not me that goes under and has to visit the loony bin. The headteacher here is wet behind the ears. So are the Education Authority types. They've no idea what goes on here and have no wish to know. I can't understand why the cane was ever banned'.

(b) After they have written their speech, read it out and tried to memorise it ask pupils to get into role and walk around the corridors of a tough secondary school, working in pairs again. The young teacher says very little. The older teacher does most of the talking – as in the poem. Use as many of the expressions as you can remember from the poem and make up your own. Basically, the older teacher is showing the young one the ropes or what he/she thinks of as being the ropes.

(c) Still in the same pairs, pupils should walk round the corridors in exactly the same way, only this time the older teacher mimes talking. We hear no sound coming from the older teacher and the younger teacher speaks his/her thoughts and reactions to what the older teacher has been saying.

(d) Now pairs should improvise a scene in which the young teacher tells the older teacher that what he/she has been saying is a load of rubbish and it's because he/she has been teaching for far too long and has become jaundiced and cynical, no longer having any point of contact with the kids and that it's about time he/she retired.

7. The above is a kind of imaginative reproduction of the scene in the poem. This is valid, but now let's move on to further scenes in which the theme is still going to be discipline, because it is a very far-reaching subject and it is possible to bring up dozens of situations in which discipline plays an important part. Do ask the GCSE group for their own thoughts on this. They will probably come up with their own ideas for scenes, but here are a few which I've tried out and which have worked very well:

(a) In groups of four. The characters are: a strict teacher, the head, a first-year pupil, a trainee teacher. The strict teacher is being told off by the head about an incident in which physical violence was used against a fourth-year pupil. The headteacher says that it is now against the law to lay a hand on any pupil and that the 'good old days' of caning are long gone. The strict teacher denies that there was any violence and the head calls in a witness, a very shy first-year pupil who happened to turn the corner at just the right time. The strict teacher yells at the first-year pupil, calling him/her a liar. The head then says 'I hope you won't call an adult member of staff a liar too'. The head then calls in the young trainee teacher who was also a witness to the incident. The strict teacher is given a warning by the head.

(b) Using the same characters as above, pupils can devise a scene or scenes in which the very strict teacher's behaviour is seen in a good light, i.e. he or she commits an act of heroism, whereas the inexperienced teacher's lax attitude to discipline leads to a disruption in which a pupil is tragically killed.

For all the above, a reading of Alan Bleasdale's play *No More Sitting on the Old School Bench* (Heinemann) would be helpful.

Further development

1. As a follow-up to this work on discipline, I'd recommend an essay to get pupils' thoughts straight: 'Why is it necessary to have self-discipline in Drama?'

2. The following pair-work situations can also work well:
   (a) A sports coach tries to explain the value of self-discipline in a particular sport. The pairs can choose any sport they like.
   (b) A master chef in conversation with a young waiter about the importance of getting the recipe right.
   (c) An older man/woman who remembers the Second World War talking to a young person about discipline in schools today.
   (d) A conversation between a judge who believes in capital punishment and a young lawyer who disagrees. The judge believes that the contemporary disease of 'boredom in the young' springs from a lack of self-discipline.
   (e) Two burglars discuss the importance of self-discipline in a successful burglary.

31 His case is typical

His case is typical.
On leaving school he showed no tendency to seek
honest employment.
I visited him often.
I formed the impression that he was not
Inherently vicious. However,
during his formative years something had snapped.

He thought everyone was against him.
He took a dislike to his Chaplain.
He failed to draw strength from the Bible.

Though the guards showed him nothing but kindness,
he made no attempt to lighten their task.
He sulked. He was bitter.

And on the last day when the privilege to choose
a reasonable menu is given to those who must die,
he neglected the offer.
He sat saying nothing.
I asked him to listen. I said to him: lad,
wait till the cyanide egg hits the acid,
then draw a deep breath;
trying to help him in spite of his coldness.
Next day I had a visit from his mother.
You were doing no more than your duty, Governor.
You did your best. You have his mother's thanks.
Your boy was one of my failures, Ma'am.
How could he think the world was against him
with someone like you at his back?

From 'New Numbers 1969' in *Ode to the Dodo* by Christopher Logue
  (Jonathan Cape)

TEACHER'S NOTES

1. The leading character need not be male.

2. As with all these text stimuli, pupils will require help mainly with structuring ideas. Groups of four or five would be best.

3. Here is a suggested framework for a prepared improvisation based on the text. The improvisation can then be scripted by the group or by one of the people in the group.

Scene 1: Scene between X and headteacher on the last day of school. Head sitting in office, door opens and in comes X. As it's the last day, anything goes and X has decided to speak his/her mind about school. Pupils should work towards a line or an action which creates a definite ending to the scene.

Scene 2: A scene at X's home. X feels isolated in the home environment. Why? What kind of attention does X receive from parents? Is there a father? Perhaps there is a younger brother or sister who is the favourite. Pupils should build the scene around an object bought for the young child (a BMX, personal stereo, computer). Again, the scene should end on a pre-arranged line or action.

Scene 3: X is now in prison. He/she has presumably killed someone. Who? X can be in a straightjacket, with the prison governor reading the statement made by X when arrested. This could actually be written out and read. X is silent throughout.

Scene 4: A scene between X and a prisoner who wants to be friends. X does not want to share any memories or objects or jokes or food. X is silent throughout.

Scene 5: Conversation between prison chaplain and the governor about X. X has been silent for at least a week, showing no inclination for work or conversation or food.

Scene 6: Solo monologue for X. X scripts his/her own speech explaining the reason for killing the victim; how, why and when it happened, in very distanced non-emotional language. At least one minute.

Scene 7: Scene between X and chaplain. Chaplain tries to draw X into conversation about religion. The execution date is mentioned. Chaplain says parent wants to see X. X refuses. Chaplain leaves the Bible with X.

Scene 8: Two guards who know X in the prison and who know he/she is going to be executed soon try to show kindness by offering to bring cigarettes.

32 You will be hearing from us shortly

You feel adequate to the demands of this position?
What qualities do you feel you
Personally have to offer?
                                        Ah
Let us consider your application form.
Your qualifications, though impressive, are
Not, we must admit, precisely what
We had in mind. Would you care
To defend their relevance?
                                        Indeed
Now your age. Perhaps you feel able
To make your own comment about that,
Too? We are conscious ourselves
Of the need for a candidate with precisely
The right degree of immaturity.
                                        So glad we agree
And now a delicate matter: your looks.
You do appreciate this work involves
Contact with the actual public? Might they,
Perhaps, find your appearance
Disturbing?
                                        Quite so
And your accent. That is the way
You have always spoken, is it? What
Of your education? Were
You educated? We mean, of course,
Where were you educated?
                                        And how
Much of a handicap is that to you,
Would you say?
                                        Married, children,
We see. The usual dubious desire
To perpetuate what had better

Not have happened at all. We do not
Ask what domestic disasters shimmer
Behind that vaguely unsuitable address.
And you were born – ?
                                    Yes. Pity.

So glad we agree.

From *Selected Poems* by U.A. Fanthorpe (Peterloo Poets)

TEACHER'S NOTES

1. Ask the class to get into pairs, give them a copy of the poem and then
   when they've read it through say that you're going to give them some job
   situations for which they are going to have to hold interviews. One of
   them is to be interviewer first, then they change over. Here are some job
   adverts which can be transferred on to cards and given out to the various
   groups:

   (a) Audio secretary. Full time, competent audio secretary required by
       local solicitor. Interview by appointment;
   (b) Dental receptionist (part-time) required for practise in central
       location. Experience of word-processing helpful;
   (c) Evening cleaners required for railway station. 1½ hours per evening
       within a new office complex. A high standard of work will be
       expected, good rates of pay;
   (d) Junior secretary required to assist company secretary with the running
       of the office. The successful applicant will need initiative and have a
       conscientious approach. Numeracy and typing skills are required, as
       are a good telephone manner and the willingness to operate the latest
       in modern office equipment. Salary is dependent upon age and
       experience;
   (e) Mature responsible person required to look after three children aged
       under six. Afternoons only, five days a week from September. Must
       have experience with children and be a car driver;
   (f) Minerva requires bright and cheerful sales assistant with a keen
       interest in selling fashion shoes and accessories;
   (g) Reliable person required to run the computerised accounting system
       for an expanding rural-based firm. Own transport essential. Good
       salary to right person;
   (h) Second chef required for busy pub restaurant, five-day week, split
       shifts, live in or out, pay negotiable;
   (i) Two company directors require housekeeper. Cleaning, some ironing,

six hours per week, flexible, good rates, references required;

(j) Tax officer. If you have initiative, commitment, an enquiring mind and leadership qualities, we can offer you a responsible and challenging career in the world of taxation. Candidates should be over 17½ and under 50 and must have at least five acceptable GCSE passes. Starting salaries from £6165p.a.

Pupils should prepare each interview as thoroughly as they can by selecting the answers they think will get them the job.

2. The class should now get into groups of three: two interviewers and an applicant. Explain that the interviewers are not very friendly, in fact they are decidedly bigoted and prejudiced because the applicant has obviously not got the right kind of background for this job. Pupils should ask themselves the following questions: What kind of job might be referred to in the poem? In which jobs is it important to have a good accent? What is meant by a good accent? Why is it important to have gone to certain schools and not to others? Is where someone is educated really important? The interviewers should adopt the same kind of prejudice as is in the poem and try to construct an interview where it is clear that either accent or class or the right address is more important than ability. The groups should work on any of the following stimuli:

(a) Interview for a receptionist's job at the BBC conducted by two BBC executive types. They should write down questions on a piece of paper, making them as personal and opinionated as possible, and try hard to test the patience of the applicant. The applicant must keep his or her cool throughout;

(b) Interview for a shop assistant in a very pukka shoe shop in Bond Street. The applicant has a distinct regional accent – either cockney or northern or Welsh, etc. The interviewers must get the applicant to give a practical demonstration of how he or she would talk to the public;

(c) Interview for a job as a courier with a top travel agency dealing in exclusive tours for very important people. Appearance, accent, qualifications, etc. are a priority with the interviewers. They ask the applicant, amongst other things, to take part in a role play where he or she must pretend that a member of the royal family or the prime minister has come into the office to book a holiday;

(d) Interview for a job with a top jeweller dealing with film stars, wealthy Arabs, American millionaires, etc. In the course of the interview the applicant has to 'act out' his/her reactions to certain people coming in. One of the interviewers is the film star, the Arab, etc.;

(e) Interview for a job as a guide in an English stately home. The applicant is expected to be a certain type and 'on paper' has all the right qualifications, background, etc. However, he/she is black – either West Indian or African, etc. He/she has no trace of a foreign accent. The interviewers reveal their prejudice when they see the applicant for the very first time.

3. Ask pupils to consider the following statement from the Sex Discrimination Act: 'No job advertisement which indicates or can reasonably be understood as indicating an intention to discriminate on grounds of sex (e.g. by inviting applications only from males or from females) may be accepted.'

Ask them to make a list of any jobs they feel men can do better than women and any they feel women can do better than men. Working in groups of four they should select a job they think would best be done by a woman and a job they think would best be done by a man. They should then interview a girl for the man's job and a boy for the woman's job. The three interviewers must not reveal any discrimination and must treat the application seriously. If pupils cannot think of any jobs themselves they could try some of the following:

- a woman as an oil rigger;
- a woman as a mechanic;
- a woman as a camera'man';
- a woman as a football player;
- a woman as as plasterer;
- a man as a flower arranger;
- a man as a nurse;
- a man as as perfume salesman;
- a man as a baby minder;
- a man as a midwife.

Further development

1. Groups can now work on a scene in which 'discrimination' plays a major part. There is one interviewer for a television discussion programme and three members of the public who are asked for their opinions on 'discrimination' in employment. The interviewer can ask the following questions:

- Is it not madness to expect women to cope with what are obviously men's jobs? For example, coal mining?

- Surely men cannot be expected to be as good as women in jobs which involve looking after young children?
- Is it not more important to look at discrimination on the grounds of race rather than sex? Or on the grounds of having the wrong accent? Or of wearing the wrong school tie?
- What is the most insidious form of prejudice?

Each member of the group must prepare a written statement on the theme of discrimination and explain what his/her conclusions are and what he/she has learnt from the drama session. Each then has to read out the statement to an imaginary television camera.

Visual stimuli

33 General approach to visual stimuli

Make as many photocopies of the visual stimuli as are necessary for the size of class and take them into the lesson with you. There is no need for each pupil to have a copy but make sure there is at least one copy for each group.

Ask the class to get into groups of four or five and to sit in their separate groups around the hall or studio. If there's an odd number, then the teacher could possibly work with that group to make up the numbers (provided it's only a small part!). Before giving out the visual stimuli say something like this:

> I'm going to give each group a picture – the same picture for all the groups – and you're going to base an improvisation on it. There is no set formula for this kind of work. There are no right answers and no wrong answers. What each group develops will be right for that group. Try not to listen to or look at or be influenced by another group's work. Your ideas will be just as valid as any other group's.

> First of all look at the picture and discuss with your group what you think the picture represents. Some pictures will be obvious; others will not. Remember, you cannot be wrong. Any ideas you have, share them. Don't keep any ideas to yourself, even if you think they're silly. Your idea might provide the starting point.

> When you're agreed upon the situation that the picture represents, start to think about characters that could possibly be in the scene. Talk about the characters and decide who is going to play which part. Try to make the characters as sharply defined and as contrasted as possible e.g. make one old, one young; one can be clever, the other dull; one can come from a totally different kind of background from the others, and so on. You decide with your group.

> When you've got your situation and your characters, then start to create a simple story line which has a definite conclusion. By this time you should have started to rehearse in role and begun to experiment with

dialogue. Make suggestions at various points as to story development and the direction in which the scene is going.

If you have a definite ending in mind, you'll find it easier because you'll have something to work towards. If not, don't worry because an ending might suggest itself as you're rehearsing.

Go for simplicity. Don't over-complicate the story. You are not necessarily restricted to one scene. You can create three or four scenes, each in a different location, if you wish, but don't have too many scenes – this is not a film or a television series.

Another tip I'd like to give you is not to have too much physical action like fights, car chases and things like that. You should essentially rely upon the spoken word. That is most important to remember. Use *words* and *dialogue* as your means of communication. We haven't got the resources of a big film company – so no stunt work!

Speak, argue, persuade, threaten, shout, whisper, explain, communicate! *Communicate with words* . . . OK? Now I'm going to give out the picture to each group and you can start planning straightaway.

When you have given out the visual stimuli, look and see which groups are finding it difficult. Go over and help them but try not to impose your ideas upon them. *Ask questions instead. Try to elicit ideas from them.* Only if it becomes patently obvious that they're never going to get started should you make a positive suggestion.

Most groups will need help with structuring their ideas and this is where the drama teacher's superior knowledge of technique will be of most use to the pupils. If they have too many scenes or are making the story too complicated or are planning meaningless fight scenes, point out that this will lead to their work being boring, repetitive or confusing to the audience. Always give a reason for what you are saying.

Ask them questions if they're stuck for ideas. Don't make statements about what you think they should do. Get them to ask themselves questions like: Why? Where? Who? Which one? When? How? What? As they get used to this kind of work, they'll get better.

I've always found that pupils like to see each other's work so try to plan the lesson so there is time for everyone to do this at the end. Establish an order of performance by letting a representative of each group select a numbered card which you've made out beforehand.

Right. OK. Now we're ready to see the results of your labours. Group one will perform their scene first, then group two, and so on. Everybody be quiet and listen and watch. You'll want others to watch you when it's your turn, so it's only fair to watch others quietly. Good audience, good performers. Bad audience, bad performers. Right. Group one. Off you go.

34 Waving to a train

QUESTIONS

1. Where is the setting for this picture? The town? The country?

2. What period is it? Modern? 1950s? 1940s? What kind of train is it?

3. Do the people in the picture belong to one family? Why is the child on the train going away? Where to? With whom?

4. As it looks like a first-class carriage, can we assume that the people are fairly well off?

5. What time of day is it? Did they have to get up early to see the young child off? Have you ever had to get up early to catch a train? How did you feel? Do you wake up easily in the morning? Do you have any breakfast? Are you in a good mood?

6. Imagine the young child on the train has been on holiday with the family and is now going back home. What kind of holiday was it? A holiday in the country? In the town? Abroad? In France? Did the children get on or did they have arguments? What time of year is it? What did they do?

7. Imagine the person on the train is going off to boarding school and it's the first time he/she has been away from home. How does he/she feel inside? How does the father feel? The mother? Has the child got a packed lunch? What kind of school is the child going to? A strict school? Is it expensive? Can the parents afford it? Why are they sending the child away?

8. Could it be that the child is going to join the mother because the parents are separating? If it's a broken home why are some children staying with the father? Do the children have a choice? What was the cause of the break up?

IDEAS

1. Theme of 'Evacuees'. During the second world war many children were sent to the country away from the big cities to avoid Hitler's bombs. Work on a scene in which the parents announce to the children that they will have to be sent away for their own safety. What ages are the children? Decide for yourselves, but don't make them too young. What does the father do for a living? The mother? Do all the children want to go away? Is it all a big adventure for them? Have they ever lived in the country before? Seen a cow? Which cities were bombed during the war? Was it dangerous? What happens when the evacuees get to their destination? What do they do all day? Have lessons? Is it boring? Does one of the children run away? Back to town? Is father furious? Does mother say the child can stay?

2. Theme of 'Holiday'. The child waving goodbye in the picture has just spent a few weeks with the family. What happened? Did they all have an enjoyable time? Are they glad to see the back of him/her? Why?

3. Theme of 'Going off to School'. It's the end of the holidays and the school term starts. Is the boy/girl going back to boarding school? Or is it a new school? Never been there before? Doesn't know anybody? What kind of people are there? Bullies? Nice people? Does the child write home to his/her parents? Are the teachers nice? Horrid? Is the child victimised? Clever?

35 Two waiters

QUESTIONS

1. Where are the two waiters? In England? Abroad? If abroad, do they speak English?

2. What kind of restaurant is it? Big? Small? A bar? A fish restaurant? A smart restaurant? A corner café?

3. How long have they been waiting? Why is it so quiet? Did somebody die in their restaurant and people hear about it?

4. What time of day is it? What season of the year?

5. Do they play music in this restaurant? Is there a band? What kind of music do they play? Classical? Jazz? Pop? A string quartet? Gypsy violins?

6. Has there been a nuclear holocaust? Is there a football match on somewhere and are they waiting for the customers to arrive?

7. If it's abroad, could the people be at a bullfight? Are the waiters used to this waiting around every day? Are they bored? What do they talk about to pass the time?

8. Are they perhaps looking across the square towards a rival café or restaurant where everyone is gathered? Why is this other restaurant attracting so many people? Why is this one so dead?

IDEAS

1. Get into pairs. You are two waiters or waitresses waiting for customers. You are both rather bored and underpaid by your very mean boss. You are speaking about all the things you'd like to do instead of waiting around here. Suddenly you are inundated by a crowd of people who have just come out of a cinema or a concert and you are propelled into frenetic activity. You'll have to imagine what the customers are saying to you. Try

to carry on the conversation with your fellow waiter/waitress while serving customers.

2. Get into threes. You are two very lazy waiters/waitresses who have joined the staff of a very busy café. You are standing around chatting when your very tyrannical boss comes in. The boss tells you what he/she expects, how to address customers, how to carry dishes, how to lay the knives and forks, how to lay the tablecloths, how to walk properly, how to speak to different kinds of customers, how to be polite when people are asking about something on the menu, how to make up the bill, etc. In other words, the boss is a tartar and you hate him/her but . . . he/she is the boss. The boss insists on a rehearsal of everything he/she has taught you. He/she plays the part of a customer.

3. Groups of three. Two waiters/waitresses are waiting and talking about the arrival of a famous film star. The third person is the film star. Whatever the waiters say about the film star is true. For example, if the waiters say that the film star walks with a limp then when the third person comes in he or she must limp in, etc. After the film star you could try another scene, waiting for (a) a member of the royal family; (b) a politician; (c) a sporting personality; (d) a television personality.

4. The two waiters/waitresses are foreigners, either French, Spanish or Italian and they are waiting for a coach party of British tourists who have booked the entire restaurant. In the end only two British tourists turn up, saying that the rest have all got tummy bugs and have retired to bed. The waiters pretend that they speak no (or very little) English in order to see what the English people will say about them. The English people are not very complimentary about the food but the waiters pretend that they can't understand English or they take the insults as praise. In the end, to get their own back, they charge an enormous bill and ask for the money in English!

5. Suggested further reading: *The Dumb Waiter* by Harold Pinter (Methuen).

36 The door in the wall

QUESTIONS

1. Where does the door lead to? A prison? A castle?

2. Is someone going to come out? Or go in?

3. Which period? Medieval? Present day?

4. What happens in the courtyard in the foreground?

5. Could it be a private house? A public building? The side door of a big house? The servants' quarters? Could it be a library? A museum? A pub? Could it be a torture chamber? Dracula's castle? A haunted house?

6. Is someone looking out through the door? Who? Why?

7. Could it be a film set? What's the film called? What's the location? Where are the people? Why is it empty?

8. How does the door open? With a big old-fashioned key? A yale lock? Does it just push open? Could there be a garden behind the door? A park?

9. Is it a magic door which leads to the 'other world'?

IDEAS

1. Rehearse a scene at a door, with someone:
   (a) listening;
   (b) shouting at someone inside;
   (c) trying to break in;
   (d) persuading someone to come out.

2. A person whose car has broken down nearby knocks on the door. It is midnight.

3. A prisoner is led through the door – either outwards to freedom or inwards to imprisonment.

4. Someone tries to enter through the door illegally.

5. Someone is waiting outside the door because his/her key won't work. The door won't budge.

6. Here are some possible starting lines:

    (a) 'Let me in';
    (b) 'Let me out';
    (c) 'We'll never get through that';
    (d) 'My best friend's through there';
    (e) 'Listen, can you hear something?';
    (f) 'Is there anybody there?';
    (g) 'Cooeeee!';
    (h) 'Don't you remember me?';
    (i) 'The last time I saw them they disappeared through that door';
    (j) 'And Merlin said, "Behind the first door there is another, and behind the second there is a third . . . until you get to the seventh door which hides the great secret . . . ".'

7. In groups of four or five work on a scenario in which a door is the most important dramatic factor. One of you is a scientist working on a top-secret formula behind locked doors. Every time you use the door you have to unbolt eight bolts and use five keys, etc. The door is also computerised and nobody can get in or out without a special pass. One day the scientist leaves his pass in the loo . . .

OR

Set up a hotel corridor with chairs to indicate doors, and possibly a lift as well. Plan a silent film mime. A man takes his girlfriend to a hotel, they come up in the lift and disappear into a room. The man's wife comes up in the lift with her boyfriend and they disappear through another door. The man comes out of his room to go to the bathroom and bumps into his wife who has come out of her room to go to the bathroom. How do they react?

37 The operation

QUESTIONS

1. Who is the person being operated on? Has he/she had an accident? A car smash? A motorcycle race which ended in disaster? Is he/she an innocent bystander? The victim of a bomb outrage?

2. How old are the doctors? What kind of training do you need to qualify as a doctor or surgeon? What is an anaesthetist? Is this a job in which concentration is important or can you have a sandwich while performing an operation?

3. Do doctors and surgeons have a difficult time? Why?

4. Is the casualty department of a hospital busy at certain times only? All the time?

5. Why do surgeons wear masks? Can they speak while they have their masks on? If not, how can they communicate with each other?

6. How do you think a doctor or surgeon feels if a patient dies?

7. Are doctors and surgeons and nurses just ordinary people? Do we regard them as such when we're in hospital? Or do we think of them as having magic powers?

8. Hospitals are very popular places in which to set dramas, especially on television. Why do you think this is so?

IDEAS

1. Get into groups of four or five. You are all surgeons performing an important operation on a boy who has had his leg smashed in a motorcycle accident. The boy is losing a lot of blood and you have to perform an operation quickly. Without any talking at all – but you are allowed some sound effects – work together to save the boy's life, but

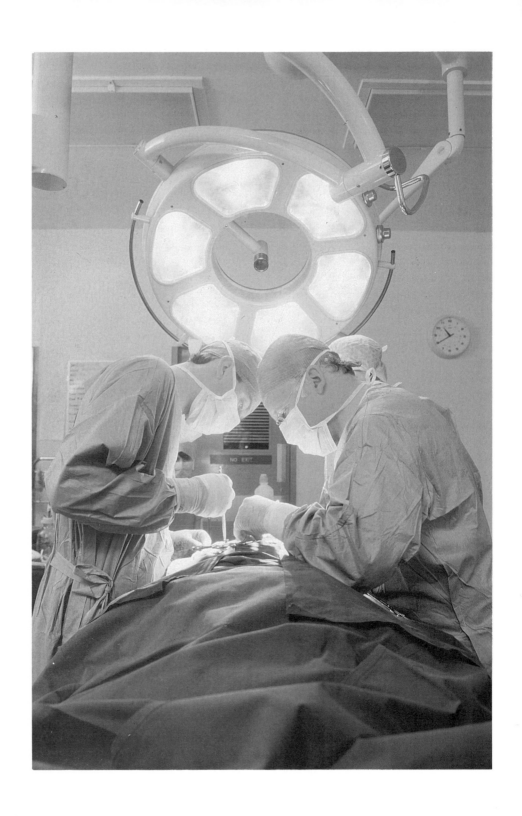

remember, no talking, everything in mime. I'll be looking for the group with the strongest concentration and sense of dramatic urgency.

2. In groups of five work on the following story. A plumber who is a bit of a bodger has just completed work putting in a bathroom at a doctor's house. The plumber says everything is fine. When the doctor runs the tap a leak springs under the bath, water pours downstairs and ruins her expensive Indian rug which cost £1000. The plumbing bill came to £500 and she has paid the plumber in cash. The doctor phones the plumber and complains about the burst pipe. The plumber says he is too busy to come out and suggests the doctor gets another plumber as he has finished the job.

Next day the doctor goes into work as usual and tells the assistant nurse about the horrid incident. The nurse says she's had the same problem and they discover that it's the same plumber. The nurse tells the hospital surgeon about it and it turns out that the surgeon also had the same problem with the same plumber a few months back. The surgeon tells the hospital chief about it and discovers that he also had the same problem a year ago.

Next day the plumber comes into casualty with a hurt thumb. How do the hospital staff get their own back on the unfortunate plumber?

3. A 'hypochondriac' is a person who is always imagining he/she is ill and who likes to talk about illness a great deal. Many doctors have to listen to these people at length. Devise a scene in pairs in which one of you is the doctor and the other is the patient. Starting line: 'I can find nothing wrong with you Mr/Mrs Smith'.

4. In groups of four work on a scene in which the following action takes place. One of you is on the operating table being given an anaesthetic before an appendix operation. As soon as you are under the anaesthetic you float out of your body and, amazingly, can witness your own operation. Of course, the surgeons can't see or hear you but you are definitely present at your own operation and silently show your reactions. Develop with the sound effect of breathing and slow-motion movement.

38 Women searching

QUESTIONS

1. Where are the women? What are they looking at? Is it a rare flower? A hole in the ground? A toad?

2. Are the women in their own private garden or are they in a public park? What are they out to do? Have they lost something? A ring? A watch? Perhaps one of the women has lost her glasses and is as blind as a bat without them.

3. Could the women be looking at a dead animal? A cat? A fish? A fox?

4. Why is this place deserted? What time of day is it?

IDEAS

1. Get into pairs. Come to an agreement about something you have lost. It could be one of you that's lost it and the other helping to look for it, or something that belongs to you both.

   Don't tell the other groups what it is you've lost. Eventually we are all going to watch each other searching and must guess what each pair is looking for by the way they are looking.

   No talking. All mime and concentration. I shall say 'Search' and you start searching. Then I'll say 'Find' and you find what it is you've been searching for. You pick it up or hold it up or do something in mime to indicate what it is you've found. We have to guess what it is.

2. Get into groups of four. You have to work on and rehearse an improvisation in which you are searching for a person in your group. This person started out with you but then mysteriously vanished. You could all have been out for a walk, pot-holing, rock climbing, visiting a fairground, dancing in a disco or just getting on a train. Somehow this person has disappeared and you have to find him/her.

   Then do another improvisation in which you lose something which is

valuable to you all – a common article, something as opposed to someone. It could be a sports cup which you've all won and is now lost or a golden disc which you've been awarded as a pop group.

What differences do you notice between the behaviour of the people in the two improvisations?

3. We're now going to do some solo mime work, with you all looking for the following things as I call them out:

needle;   glasses;
kite;   pencil case;
keys;   cassette;
jumper;   rubber;
watch;   helicopter.

Now search and call for the following:

your cat;
your mother;
your headteacher;
the caretaker;
God;
the police.

4. Suppose women in the picture are trespassing. In groups of three work out an improvisation in which two of you are trespassing somewhere and the other person finds you out.

39 The staircase

QUESTIONS

1. What kind of house do you think this is? A spooky house? A museum? A stately home? A house in the country?

2. Who lives in this house? A family? An old man or woman alone? A group of squatters? Nobody at all?

3. Where does the door lead to? A bedroom? A large sitting room with an enormous log fireplace at the other end?

4. Is there anybody in the room? Hiding? A person with his/her back to the door as you go in? What kind of face does he/she have when he/she turns round?

5. Is the house inhabited? Are there cobwebs? Is somebody about to come out of the door? Who? Is somebody coming up the stairs?

6. What time of day is it?

7. Is something going on downstairs? Perhaps someone can come out on to the landing and listen to what is going on downstairs? Are there funny noises in this house? Creaks? Ghostly voices?

IDEAS

1. In pairs devise a conversation in which two young people are listening from the landing to what is going on downstairs. Starting line: 'Can you hear what they're saying now?'

2. In groups of four, develop an improvisation around the theme of a deserted house. Two young people are exploring the countryside when they come across an old deserted house. They peer in through the windows and are amazed to see that the house looks as if it is lived in but there is in fact not a soul around. They hear strange sounds coming from upstairs and decide to go up the staircase. At the top of the stairs they

notice a door is ajar and that is where the strange noises are coming from. What do they do? Finish the improvisation off. You could add two more characters.

3. Work in your groups on a filmscript with the theme of a 'spooky' house. Here is the suggested storyline:

Scene one: A couple of young children from the town are visiting their uncle and aunt who live in the middle of nowhere, right out in the country. They ask if they can go exploring and their aunt says yes, but not to go near the deserted house because it's supposed to be haunted.

Scene two: The children are outside the deserted house and they decide to go in (sound effect – creaking door). They describe what they see as they go from room to room. Cobwebs everywhere? Rats? They see an old staircase and walk up (sound effect – creaking steps). At the top of the stairs they notice a door ajar and a strange light coming from the room behind as if there is a fire lit. They go in and, to their amazement, see an old lady in a rocking chair sitting by the fire. She bids them come in and is very friendly. She makes them a cup of tea and gives them some home-made cake. She says she's lived in this house for seventy years but not many people know she's still alive. They all think she's dead and the house is deserted but it's not true, as they can see.

Scene three: The children go back home to their uncle and aunt and tell them their adventures. The uncle and aunt say the old lady is definitely dead because she's buried in the churchyard.

Scene four: At the churchyard. They see the old lady's tombstone.

Scene five: They return to the deserted house and find not a trace of a human being. The room at the top of the stairs contains the rocking chair but no old lady.

You could devise an alternative surprise ending yourselves.

40 The trunk

QUESTIONS

1. Whom does the trunk belong to? What is in it? Where is it going?

2. Are the two people in the train husband and wife? Who is the third gentleman sitting behind them?

3. Is this a modern train? Do we have third class carriages today? How is the train powered? Coal? Steam? Electricity?

4. What kind of sound does this train make? Do you think the sound of the train could be a dramatic factor in the story you are going to evolve? Do you know any plays or films set on a train?

5. Of the two porters, is one of them the chief porter?

6. What time of day is it? Is this a long or short journey for the people on the train? Do they all know each other?

IDEAS

1. Get into groups of five and develop a story based on the characters you see in the picture. It would be effective to have a train 'sound track' in the background. Either get a loop or make one up of a train in motion and one of you can operate it during the performance.

2. If you can obtain a 'prop' trunk it would be very helpful. Remember to 'mime' heaviness and weight when lifting the trunk.

3. The porters may have different accents from the people in the train. The accents would pinpoint the place in which the action is taking place.

4. Here is a suggested scenario:

   Scene one: Two porters are in their office moaning about the amount of work they have to do and how heavy people's luggage seems to be

153

nowadays. Make a contrast between the two porters (e.g. one might be old and the other young). A rich-looking gentleman comes into the office and asks them if they would be kind enough to unload a trunk from his car (or carriage?) which is to travel on the 3.15 to (Birmingham?).

Scene two: The porters unload the trunk from the car (or carriage) and wheel it to the train, grumbling all the time about how heavy it is and how little they get paid. A lady joins the gentleman and they get on to the train asking the porters to handle the trunk with care as it contains valuable items of rare (antiques? books? glass? china?). The gentleman gives the porters a huge tip which sends them into paroxysms of thanks.

Scene three: The train is in motion (so remember to act as if you are moving on a train) and the lady and gentleman are talking about how clever they have been in getting the two porters to load the trunk on the train. A mysterious person asks if he/she can join them. He/she is also travelling to (Birmingham?). This stranger admires the trunk and asks what is in it. The husband/wife replies that it contains valuable household items.

Scene four: One of the porters comes along the corridor and announces that it is time for lunch. The couple and the mysterious stranger go off to the restaurant car. The inquisitive porter decides to have a look in the trunk and, with much difficulty, manages to open it. He realises now why it was so heavy: it contains (gold bars? a body?). He is about to leave when the gentleman returns with the lady. He points a gun at the porter and is about to shoot him when the mysterious person (who is in fact a policeman!) appears from behind with another gun.

Supply an ending and an explanation for what is in the trunk.

41 Policeman – street scene

• Age range: 13–16

QUESTIONS

1. Has the young man done something to make the policeman stop? Why are they in conversation? Has the young man stopped the policeman to tell him something?

2. What is the young man holding in his hand? A drink? A can of beer? Is he drunk? Was he being a nuisance to passing pedestrians? Did a passing pedestrian go and get the policeman?

3. What is the young man's background? A down-and-out? From a good home? On drugs? What is he doing in the city? Is it a city?

4. Has the young man got any friends? Where are they? Where does he live? With his parents? Or has he run away from home? Is he staying with friends? Dossing?

5. Look at his clothes. Is he wearing walking gear? Is he camping? Who with? Where? Is he a student? Is he on holiday?

6. What about the policeman? Is he a typical bobby? Does he like his job? Is he friendly or aggressive towards the young man? How long has he been a policeman? Did he ever want to be anything else? What's his name? What's the name of the young man?

IDEAS

1. Create new characters in addition to the policeman and the young man. What are their names and how old are they? What relationship do they have to the two in the picture?

2. The young man is a plain clothes police officer. He is trying to break a drugs ring in this town. He can't tell the policeman because it'll blow his cover.

3. The policeman is the young man's father. Discuss the family background and enact a scene at home which will give a clue as to the reason for the young man's drunken behaviour. Is there a mother or not?

(As a lead up to this idea (or instead of it) try an improvisation about a school teacher whose son/daughter goes to the same school where she/he teaches. What kind of favouritism is shown, if any?)

4. The young man has just won the pools and is celebrating. Or is it Cup Final Day? The young man is the son of a very famous person. The policeman doesn't believe him.

5. The young man is a foreigner and doesn't speak English.

6. Here are some possible starting lines:
    (a) 'It wasn't me, guv'. It was that bloke over there';
    (b) 'How old are you, son? Is that alcohol you're drinking?';
    (c) 'Don't pick on me, just because I look a bit rough';
    (d) 'This is a free country';
    (e) 'You're showing me up, son';
    (f) 'You don't believe who my dad is, do you?';
    (g) 'I'll tell you who did it, officer';
    (h) 'I'm getting sick and tired of you, son'.

42 Shop premises to let • Age range: 14–16

QUESTIONS

1. What kind of shop do you think this would make? A restaurant? A bookshop? A curtain shop? A toy shop?

2. Who actually owns the building? Is this person a good or a bad landlord/landlady? Will he/she charge a lot of money to rent out the premises? Is he/she greedy?

3. What kind of area do you think this is? Is it a rich area or a poor area or a fairly middle-of-the-road area? What kind of business would do well in this area? Are there any businesses that do well no matter what the area? How about a video hire shop?

4. What sort of people are going to rent the shop premises? Are they going to be a family with children? A married couple without children? A single person? A consortium of businessmen?

5. Have they had a shop before or is this their first venture?

6. What kind of shop was it before?

7. Are there many repairs to be done before they can open the shop? Have they bought their stock yet? Where do they get it from?

8. Do any 'dramas' take place in shops? Theft? Pickpockets? Loss of property? Forgetting a purse on the counter? Conflict of personalities? Rudeness to customers?

IDEAS

1. The whole class can work on this picture together, or just half the class. First of all decide what kind of shop you are going to have. Having decided that, you must then allocate parts – landlords/landladies, shopkeepers, customers, stockists, etc. Here is a simple scenario:

Scene one: A couple of people are walking past a shop and notice that it is empty and for rent. They peer inside and remember when it was a tea shop/supermarket/hardware shop or such like.

Scene two: They visit the agent to find out about the rent and who owns the property. They want to run a tea shop. They visit the landlord/landlady who normally charges a lot of money to rent the premises, but eventually lets them have it for £100 a week even though they think this is extortionate.

Scene three: They decide to do the decorations themselves and begin to tidy up the place.

Scene four: They visit various suppliers to buy things like tables, chairs, crockery, tea, cakes.

Scene five: They now have interviews to employ kitchen staff and waitresses.

Scene six: Opening day. Customers come in and are served.

The above is a framework on which to base improvisations in large groups. Choose shops which involve a lot of people coming into the shop, like a restaurant, a video hire shop, a grocery store, etc.

2. Groups of four. Choose the kind of shop you want and then take the roles of shopkeeper and three customers. Each customer has a complaint to make and the poor shopkeeper has to obey the dictum that 'the customer is always right'.

3. Groups of six: two burglars, two policemen, two shopkeepers. Develop an improvisation with the title 'Attempted Robbery'.

4. Groups of six. A shop sells factory machinery. One of the sales assistants is new and the others make fun of him/her because he/she is a bit naïve. They trick him/her into putting his/her hand into a very dangerous piece of machinery and the machine mashes him/her up. The sales assistant becomes a 'ghost' in the factory and slowly takes revenge on all the others by having them eliminated one by one. Devise your own methods of extermination. Work on machine sound effects as well.

43 Job centre

QUESTIONS

1. How long has the man been looking for work?

2. Is the white man helpful? Why?

3. What happens when the black man turns up for the interview? Has he got a chip on his shoulder? Does he think everybody is against him? Is it true, or is the black man his own worst enemy?

4. What constitutes prejudice? Have you ever encountered it? How? Where? Can you do a scene to show what you mean? Can you put it into dramatic terms?

5. Is the colour of your skin important? Do you think getting a job ought to depend upon the colour of your skin or whether you can do the job?

6. Are people trying to combat racial intolerance? Are they succeeding? Work on a scene in which a white man is trying to get a black man a job but fails. Why does he fail?

7. Does the same apply for women as for men? If you are black and a woman do you stand even less chance of getting a job?

8. Does everybody want to work or do some people fight shy of work, no matter what the colour of their skin? Devise a scene in which a person goes to a job interview and deliberately goes out of his/her way not to get the job.

9. What do you think is the basic difference between school life and work life? Is it better to remain at school to do 'A' levels or to go out and get a job? Do you really need qualifications to get a good job these days? Work on a scene in which you are discussing this very thing with your parents or your teacher.

IDEAS

1. In pairs work on a scene in which prejudice is obvious, but not admitted:

   (a) An interview for a job as a cook. The interviewer is white, polite, educated and extremely helpful. The applicant is young, black, enthusiastic about catering and has some qualifications. However, he does not get the job. Work on the characters and try to make the whole interview very courteous and low-key. Don't exaggerate or get upset. Starting line: 'Come in, Mr Johnson, I'm so glad you could make it';

   (b) You are a young black person and are looking for a room. You see an advert in a tobacconist's shop window and it's just what you're looking for. You phone up and are told the room is available. You decide to call in person and then find that the room is no longer available. On asking why, you are told that it was taken just a minute ago. Starting line: 'Is the bedsit still available?';

   (c) You are a young white person and have fallen in love with a black boy/girl. You go to tell the father or mother you'd like to get married. Starting line: 'I think you know why I've come round'.

2. Here are some starting lines for other scenes:

   (a) 'I've been waiting in this job centre for so long I'm growing a beard';

   (b) 'Is that what you call an interview suit?';

   (c) 'Hello, I'm the school careers officer. Have you any idea what job you'd like to do when you leave school?';

   (d) 'Gi's a job, mate';

   (e) 'I've got some questions to ask you about your school career';

   (f) 'My dad says it's not worth getting a job. Better to be on the dole';

   (g) 'In Panorama this evening we're going to talk to Mr Johnson who was passed over for a job as a cook in favour of a white candidate. Mr Johnson, would you like to tell us what happened at the interview?'.

44 Fumigating books

QUESTIONS

1. Is this set in the future? Or not?

2. Is there such a thing as nuclear dust? Ordinary dust gone wrong? A danger? To whom?

3. Are we on earth?

4. Can the sound of breathing be a dramatic factor in the story?

5. Is it a person in the picture? A human being? A robot? A machine?

6. Is this a library? A secret storehouse? A museum? A private dwelling? The house of a wealthy individual?

7. If the person takes off the protective covering from his/her face, what will be underneath?

8. Are the books valuable in any way?

IDEAS

1. Groups of four or five. A nuclear fallout shelter some time in the future. An underground library. The four-minute warning sounds at the start. People are gathering. There is confusion. A variety of characters: an optimist, a pessimist, a priest, a mother – look at *Character words* pages 69–70 for ideas. Amidst growing hysteria as to what has happened there is a dull explosion off. The main door closes automatically. Nobody else can come in. They have been trapped outside. The mother's child is outside. Each character speaks about people they know outside who are probably now dead. You cannot budge the door and anyhow the radiation would kill you instantly if you went out. The door to the food supply – standard in all nuclear fallout shelters – is jammed. You are trapped without food. Suddenly you hear a noise. You turn and see a

robot with a special vacuum cleaning the books in the library. What happens next?

2. Imagine you are books and stand in book shapes on shelves. Talk according to the type of book you are. Text books talk in a serious way, thrillers talk like American gangsters, gardening books talk like country yokels, etc. A cleaner comes along with a hoover to suck up the dust from you and you are all petrified of this monstrous instrument.

3. You are chatting in a library. A sound off. Weird-sounding (like breathing in a space suit). On hearing this sound you stop talking and put on radiation suits and masks – as in a ritual. You continue chatting as normal and never refer to the sound. A 'being' comes in to clean the books with a radiation instrument. It also cleans the air. The 'being' moves in slow motion. You begin to speak about the 'old days'.

4. Here are some possible starting lines:

  (a) 'It's coming for us';
  (b) 'I'm fed up with you buying all these books';
  (c) 'This is the one I'm after. See the title?';
  (d) 'Keep your eyes peeled while I poison these books';
  (e) 'Mum, what's that strange man doing in the library?'.

5. Suggested further reading: *The Genesis Roadshow* by Ian Sharp (Edward Arnold); *In Camera* by Jean-Paul Sartre (Penguin).

45 Part of a crowd

QUESTIONS

1. What are they looking at? Where are they? A pop concert? An air display?

2. Is someone talking to them from a platform? Who? Is it a political speaker perhaps? What is he or she saying? Is he/she trying to convince the crowd of something? Are the speakers standing on a 'soapbox'?

3. Is the crowd listening attentively? Are they concentrating? Does that mean they are interested in what is going on? Are they convinced by the speaker? Doubtful? Unsure?

4. Do people in a crowd think, or are they just passive listeners, almost hypnotised by whoever is speaking? Can you be an individual within a crowd?

5. Are they watching a giant screen? Are they being indoctrinated by a fanatical religious sect? Can you think of any examples in history or dramatic literature of crowds being swayed by skilled orators? What qualities do you need to be a 'charismatic' speaker?

6. Are they watching something extraordinary? An apparition? A miracle? A flying saucer landing? Or are they watching a real-life drama? Somebody on a roof threatening to jump off? Somebody being rescued by the fire brigade?

IDEAS

1. Get into groups of four or five. You are going to be part of a large crowd watching a dramatic event happening 'off stage'. A young person is threatening to jump from a window ledge at the top of a tall building. Express in mime the different emotions and reactions of a crowd watching this incident: concern, fear, horror, disbelief, terror, relief. Through your mime show what is happening off stage. Work together and aim for group awareness. You have a couple of minutes to rehearse. The end result doesn't have to last long – about a minute will do, or longer if you can

manage it. You must try to engage the attention of the audience watching you, just as a skilled speaker gains the attention of the crowd he or she is addressing. In the same groups you can also try watching:

(a) an air display at which a plane accidentally crashes;
(b) a gigantic flying saucer landing;
(c) a young child being rescued from a fire;
(d) a cat being rescued from a tall tree;
(e) a helicopter losing control and coming straight for you.

2. In your groups one of you must be 'the speaker', the person on whom the crowd is focused. Each of you must take a turn at being speaker. You have to write a speech trying to put across your point of view and attempting to convince others that your view is right. You must write at least one page. Don't tell the others what you are going to speak about, so that 'the crowd' can react naturally and spontaneously. You can talk about the virtues of one political party over another or the harmful effects of too much television-gazing or the reasons why you prefer a certain pop group to another. Anything you like – as long as you have a point of view. When you come to give your speech the other members of your group become part of the crowd listening and reacting – but they must react without sound as if someone has turned down the volume on the television. The crowd's faces react but their voices are not heard. You continue until the end of your speech watching the reactions of the crowd and responding to them. The crowd can make gestures and movements but no words.

3. In your groups work on a story line about some young people who go to an event where there is a large crowd of people. At this event one of you is robbed of some money. You tell the police but they are not interested, there is too much crime to handle that day. You go back home and dread telling your parents.

Acknowledgements

The publishers would like to thank the following for permission to reprint copyright material: John Antrobus, Trixie and Baba (John Calder); U A Fanthorpe for 'You will be hearing from us shortly' and 'Waiting Gentlewoman' from Selected Poems (Peterloo Poets); Mick Gowar 1981 for 'Teaching Practice' from So Far So Good (William Collins Sons & Co Ltd); Christopher Logue for 'New Numbers 1969' from Ode to the Dodo (Cape); Willy Russell, Our Day Out (Margaret Ramsay); Stevie Smith for 'Valuable' from Collected Poems (McGibbon).

Photographs courtesy of: Tim Beddow/Science Photo Library (p 144); P.B. Whitehouse, Colourviews (p 135); Daily Mail (p 168); David Hoffman (p 159); Anna Arnone, Photo Coop (p 168); Patricia Theodorou (pp 138, 141, 147, 150, 153, 156, 159).

Designed by Sue Lacey.
Cover design by Ned Hoste.